VOICES UNDER THE GROUND

VOICES UNDER THE GROUND

Themes and Images
in the Early Poetry of Gunnar Ekelöf

BY

ROSS SHIDELER

with a foreword by Reidar Ekner

UNIVERSITY OF CALIFORNIA PRESS
BERKELEY · LOS ANGELES · LONDON
1973

University of California Publications in Modern Philology

Volume 104

Approved for publication June 15, 1971
Issued February 5, 1973

University of California Press
Berkeley and Los Angeles
California

◊◊◊

University of California Press, Ltd.
London, England

ISBN: 0-520-09415-8
Library of Congress Catalog Card No.: 70-171620

DEDICATION

Everything I attempt that is positive must be dedicated to my parents.

Bob, Beth, and other dear friends will realize, I hope, how much they are a part of this study on the creation of poetry and the consciousness of the poet and his reader.

To SUSAN

> "Canaries in the morning, orchestras
> In the afternoon, balloons at night."

FOREWORD

GUNNAR EKELÖF, the poet to whom Ross Shideler has devoted the present study, is the most many-sided and consistent of all Scandinavian modernists and one of the most important European poets of this century.

His unique poetic talent was recognized in his native country, Sweden, as soon as he made his internationally oriented début in 1932, but it took almost twenty years for him to achieve the same recognition in the other Scandinavian countries and still another decade before his international breakthrough. At his death in 1968—he was born in 1907—his selected poems were available in most European languages, including French, German, Italian, Czech, Finnish, and English.

Ross Shideler has judiciously abstained from trying to give a complete account of Ekelöf's extensive and comprehensive writings. (In his lifetime Ekelöf published 15 independent collections of poetry and three volumes of essays. Much is written about him, and more is to follow.) With a fine sense for essentials, Shideler has instead limited his study to one of Ekelöf's most central poems, the lengthy, enigmatic, and suggestive "Voices Under the Ground," which contains a series of Ekelöf's central themes. It exists in several versions, the final one from 1951. It is a complicated, dreamlike composition, filled with unidentified dialogue and fleeting images, indirectly related to the poet's biography.

With an apt pedagogic grip, Shideler devotes his first chapter to a preliminary analysis, an enlightening close reading of the text. Using other Ekelöf texts for support, texts with similar metaphors, symbols or situations, Shideler argues that the poem consists of several levels, one more conscious and one—or several—fictitiously more unconscious levels, where the voices of dreams and the subconscious are heard. By analyzing the poem according to the laws of a musical composition, Mr. Shideler then shows how the various themes of time and man, of ideal, chaos, and death are developed within a coherent structure that mirrors the split self of a dreamer, seeking refuge or escape from a

[vii]

frustrating reality. In the center of the poem Shideler discerns archetypal images that symbolize the regression of the dreamer into a primitive inner universe of several layers (the stone, the labyrinth, the cave, and the womb). He applies the theories of such psychoanalytically oriented critics as Gaston Bachelard, Charles Baudouin, and Norman O. Brown to his interpretation, with interesting results.

In his second chapter Shideler shifts the focus to the obviously autobiographical content of the poem. Taking three autobiographical prose pieces by Ekelöf as his starting point, he uses the structural, psychological, imagistic, and thematic similarities within Ekelöf's writings as a key to the personal symbolism of "Voices Under the Ground." The theme of "death-in-life," symbolized by the stone and the voices in the poem, is traced back to the poet's childhood experience with an insane father who was nursed at home. The father sat in the apartment mumbling nonsensical words, while the little boy tried to make sense out of the letters and words in an ABC-book, unable fully to understand the connection between a letter, the picture of a dog's nose, and the nose of the family dog. Hence, Shideler calls the problematic relation between words and reality "the dognose problem." It is a main theme in Ekelöf's writing, and Shideler's analysis of it is an important contribution toward a better understanding of Ekelöf's poetic method and its foundation within the poet's childhood experience. The theme of opposing levels of reality and the problem of the unconscious, both present in "Voices Under the Ground," are also traced back to the same source. Shideler's daring suggestion, that the figure of death that appears at the end of "Voices Under the Ground" is consciously or unconsciously related to the memory of the father, is at least very seductive. Shideler convincingly interprets the father image both as an identification and a threat. That Ekelöf's themes of alienation and split personality go back to this strange father-son relationship is obvious. Shideler suggests that the young boy turned to music and poetry in order to solve the inner conflicts that resulted from these disturbing childhood experiences.

Pursuing the occurrence of the same themes and images in a few key poems, Shideler in chapter III broadens the perspective and elucidates the permanence and coherence of Ekelöf's poetic universe. Shideler shows that the transition from a conflict between dream life and conscious life to an acceptance of life in all its aspects occurs only very slowly. "In Ferry Song" (1941) Ekelöf presents his mystic conviction that there exists a third possibility, a force above the opposing forces. Ekelöf calls it the Virgin. Convinced that there is no single self, no ego, the poet accepts the voices within himself and finds in the Virgin the visionary symbol of harmony, balance, and hope. Biographically, "Voices Under the Ground" corresponds to a period preceding this development.

Ross Shideler's intelligent and stimulating analysis of Ekelöf's major poem "Voices Under the Ground" is a welcome contribution to Ekelöf scholarship and to a certain extent introduces a new way of reading and understanding his poetry. The value of Shideler's thesis lies first in its establishing of an inner relation between "Voices Under the Ground" and the poet's childhood, and second in its discovery of a close resemblance between the symbolic structure of the poem and certain archetypal structures studied by Bachelard, Baudoin, and others. By this comparative method, Shideler is able to throw new light, from an unusual angle, on Ekelöf's dream poem.

On one point, however, I have to disagree with his analysis. One of the main images of the poem, perhaps the central one, is the bird, also called Archaeopteryx. (By choosing the archetype of all birds, Ekelöf points to the archetypal pattern of the poem.) Shideler interprets the bird as a symbol of the poet's vision of the ideal. And in fact it is very likely that the bird in "Voices" symbolizes the ideal, on an abstract level. It is necessary, however, to make the interpretation more specific. To me it seems obvious that the bird is of the female sex, that it represents a beloved woman who has reluctantly abandoned the narrator for someone else, for "a new light," to use the words of the poem. The narrator is left to his loneliness and his longing for the bird, which symbolizes a lost happiness. The bird's argument, that it leaves to offer him a much greater happiness, is really, as the narrator comments, "a diplomatic fight for freedom," that is freedom *for* the bird *from* the narrator.

The interpretation of the bird as a symbol of a woman is confirmed by the poet's personal situation in 1932, when the first version of the poem was written, and later. Shideler is right, however, in stressing the archetypal character of the poem and its images. Gunnar Ekelöf transformed a personal situation into an archetypal pattern, where the bird may symbolize the ideal as well.

To follow Shideler's detailed arguments, it is necessary to be familiar with the poem and other texts by Ekelöf. All the relevant texts— most of them translated by Shideler—are to be found in the appendix.

Stockholm University   Reidar EKNER
                                                              Docent

PREFACE

GUNNAR EKELÖF is one of Sweden's major twentieth-century writers, but because of the limited number of people who read Swedish he is little known outside of his own country. Only gradually has significant criticism about Ekelöf begun to appear and all of it is in Swedish. Reidar Ekner, the major Ekelöf scholar, has published a volume of essays on Ekelöf and has just published a brilliant bibliography of his works, including criticism about his writing and translations of it. Göran Printz-Påhlson published a major critical article about Ekelöf a number of years ago, and in the last fifteen to twenty years numerous scholarly and critical articles have been written which support the general acceptance of Ekelöf's importance within the Scandinavian literary tradition.

This study is an attempt at discussing some of the major themes in the first twenty years of Ekelöf's writing, approximately 1932 to 1951. Beginning with one poem, "Voices Under the Ground," which has never been fully explained, the study circles the poem three times from different critical perspectives. The poem is then used as a fulcrum to study other writings of Ekelöf which give some insight into his childhood and his early years of writing. The concluding chapter surveys his first twenty years of poetry in light of the themes and images that have developed through the rest of the book. The translations, necessarily literal I am afraid, are my own unless otherwise indicated. "Voices Under the Ground" appears on p. 121. It should be read before starting chapter I.

Apart from my own critical deficiencies, and the limitations imposed upon me by being separated from all source material, this book may do more than a slight injustice to Ekelöf in that it does not always, nor perhaps even to a major extent, concern itself with his "best" writing, but rather with his earliest. A few of his major poems are studied here, but Ekelöf, a prolific poet and a member of the Swedish Royal Academy before he died, produced a large body of work, and some of his greatest poetry was written in the last five years of his life. Therefore, this study is humbly intended as an introduction to a poet whom I consider to be a major European writer.

A Swedish-English portion of an earlier version of the first chapter appears in the November 1970 issue of *Scandinavica,* published at Cambridge University, England.

My thanks to Ingrid Ekelöf and Albert Bonniers Publishing Company for permission to use and translate some of Ekelöf's writing, and to Twayne Publishers for permission to reprint translations from their volume *Selected Poems of Gunnar Ekelöf* (New York, 1967) with translations by Muriel Rukeyser and Leif Sjöberg.

Many people have helped me with the book in one way or another. Erik O. Johannesson helped me in my Scandinavian studies; Alain Renoir has given me professional assistance and guidance; and Jim Larson has been an important intellectual influence on me. All three of these men, to whom I am indebted, are at the University of California, Berkely, as is Josephine Miles, whose help, guidance, support, and friendship I deeply treasure. Reidar Ekner, with extraordinary generosity, has read the manuscript, made many helpful suggestions, and saved me from some grievous technical errors.

June 1967—Berkeley; June 1970—Los Angeles

My sincere apologies to Ingrid Ekelöf and Bengt Landgren, both of whom published major works on Ekelöf after my study was completed and accepted for publication. Bengt Landgren's fine book *Ensamheten, döden och drömmarna—Studier över ett motivkomplex i Gunnar Ekelöfs diktning* (Lund: Berlingska Boktryckeriet, 1971) substantiates some of my theories and reveals facts about Ekelöf's life unavailable to me. The book focuses on Ekelöf's later poetry, but it also points out the relationship between the poet's life and his writing. Ingrid Ekelöf edited and published some of her husband's papers as *Gunnar Ekelöf En självbiografi—Efterlämnade brev och anteckningar* (Stockholm: Bonniers, 1971). The two books would have been major source material for my much more limited study and I deeply regret their absence from this work.

July 1972—Los Angeles

CONTENTS

Poems and Prose by Ekelöf

I. LISTENING TO THE VOICES

"on pillows of stone, under sheets of stone."

GUNNAR EKELÖF's poem "Voices Under the Ground," published in
In Autumn (1951) has been only casually touched upon by Swedish
critics, yet it is one of Ekelöf's major poems.[1] In it many of the crucial
themes and images of the first twenty years of his poetry reach full
fruition, for, with complete technical mastery, he draws upon the
unconscious to symbolize and to identify his concern with dreams and
with man's alienated and mortal consciousness. At first this poem
seems like an incomprehensible dialogue between voices under the
ground, with some unidentified observer above the ground. Upon
further analysis, however, the poem has the unified structure of a
dream and the dialogue represents a dialogue within the narrator's own
consciousness.

This seemingly unstructured poem has a rather clear framework
that can be outlined in musical terms, but the full depth of the poem
is illuminated only when we see how Ekelöf uses symbols such as the
bird and the stone within the structure of a dream. Ultimately, the
poem deals in archetypal imagery with the narrator's lack of a space
that he can comfortably inhabit and with his ambivalence toward
death.

The origins of the poem lie within a group of poems, "Written Down
in 1932," published in *In Autumn*, and in "A Deathdream," published
in *Non Serviam* (1945). "Voices Under the Ground" was itself first
published as "The Devil's Sermon" in *Bonniers Litterära Magasin*
(*BLM*) in 1947. The development of these poems from "Written Down
in 1932" to "A Deathdream" to the final version published as "Voices
Under the Ground" gives us some idea of Ekelöf's main poetic con-

---

[1] The poem is briefly discussed in Göran Printz-Påhlson's essay "Diktarens
kringkastade lemmar" i *Solen in spegeln* (Stockholm, 1958), and Brita Wigforss's
article "Ekelöf, vid horisonten," in *BLM* (March 1963).

cerns as well as his development over this twenty-year period. Before examining the poem itself, it may be helpful to look at the earlier versions.

Ekelöf in a footnote in *In Autumn* verified that "Voices Under the Ground" is one of the poems that contains certain fundamental themes with which he had never quite finished.[2] This statement, implying that he had been working with these themes for many years, is supported by the poems, apparently almost dictated from dreams, which are published in *In Autumn* under the title of "Written Down in 1932" and originally appeared in *Bonniers Litterära Magasin* in 1951 as "Studies and Variations—Crisis Papers November 1932" in a somewhat different and rearranged form. (See p. 115 for poem.)

It is difficult to find any unifying element in "Written Down in 1932." Sleep and dreams in their relationship to life, and what may be either the narrator's experience of life or his insomnia, are the dominating subjects, but sections four and five do not support even this generalization.

The basic contradiction of whether or not the subject matter is "trivial," as the opening line suggests, is never resolved, although a contrast between life and death may be emphasized by the contradiction. The irresolution gives the first two sections a self-conscious attitude that even further interferes with the reading of the poem as a successful unity. Lines such as "I write badly . . ." and "I have suicidal dark flashes . . ." prevent the reader from becoming involved in the real problems of sleep, truth, and identity which the poet seems to want to present.

The second section begins a process of images upon which the reader may meditate, such as time, the motion of sinking, the lifeboat, and nightlessness. The "evening clouds gloria" and the "hands cut off" suggest the influence of Edith Södergran's "Landscape at Sunset." With the third section we are taken fully into an image separate from but specifically related to sleep. The stone is closed and dreams alone. From that point the narrator develops a series of images of petrification and time, of death in life, which he keeps associating effectively with his identification with the "birds" in the stone. The darkness in which

[2] Gunnar Ekelöf, *Om hösten* (Stockholm, 1951), p. 103.

he gropes evolves into an abyss or pit. There are some difficulties in understanding "the light of the abyss" or "the limestone," but the theme of sleep and darkness is more or less cohesive throughout this section.

The fourth section opens with a more self-conscious introduction, although the close personal attitude is displaced by the imagery of thirst, water, rain, and autumn. Thematically, the section seems only distantly related to the rest of the poem.

Again, with section five, the narrator speaks directly, and here he is attempting to communicate a thought process that is more complex than the emotional "forgive me" or "I am sick" attitudes. The section at midpoint returns to the imagery of night and darkness which can easily be related to section three. The conclusion of the poem seems somewhat surprising.

A general justification for the poem must lie in its spontaneity, its daydream quality, for, studying it as closely as I can, I find no visible plan that unifies it. If it has a unity, it must be an emotive one. Its symbols, such as the colors, are relatively obvious and do not arise from a development within the poem. I find section three the most unified passage with its levels of associations functioning on two planes, the horizontal—stone, sleep, death, darkness, and night —and the vertical—bird, light, pit, fish.

The next poem in the sequence leading up to "Voices Under the Ground" (hereafter called "Voices") is "A Deathdream," published in *Non Serviam* and drawn for the most part from section three of "Written Down in 1932." The most immediate thing noticeable about "A Deathdream" in comparison to the earlier poem is that it attempts to formally dominate its own structure and theme.

The poem's title defines it as occurring in the sphere of dreams. For a poem supposedly about the nonsensuous subjects of dreams and death, its appeal is markedly sensuous. The specific sense appealed to is that of touch. From the "fondle" of the first line, we are aware of the tactile quality of the poem, a quality that is sustained throughout.

The narrator identifies with the stone he touches and, perhaps, identifies the stone with himself. He describes physical sensations and the thoughts he has about them. The stone is alive for the narrator and as bird "comes back sometimes out of habit or duty." The freedom of the bird is contrasted to the narrator who is held to the stone and who becomes part of the stone. Now everything turns in him and he seems to become a part of the slow motion of the universe, "Now time turns slowly and feelinglessly around its axle." Surrounded by stone, he smothers in it, yet sees the other animals and birds within it as they apparently live within its slow pulse. With two such tactile words as "smother" and "drown," the narrator emphasizes his living death in the stone.

We are taken from the intensity of this world to the awakening of the dreamer. Is he waking up to life or to death? These lines serve to remind us that the poem is a dream, but they do not really resolve the poem nor do they contribute to the remarkable imagery of the major part of the poem.

Rationally, the poem is comprehensible to anyone who has had a dream, and it requires no special knowledge to follow it. The images are easily associated and the pattern from dream to stone to bird and back to stone and then dreamer is carefully delineated. This gives us some idea of the development of the poet between 1932 and 1945.

The poet has learned how to present a narrator and his dreamworld within a tightly organized poem. We can see what specific elements the poet sacrificed in order to do this. He must have felt it necessary to eliminate the personal element, as the narrator of "A Deathdream" is an unidentified figure whose experience of the dream is presented without additional commentary. This personal element, apart from the mention of sleep, refuge, and dreams constituted the entire first section of "Written Down in 1932" and was excluded.

The second section contained what one might call a cosmos of symbolic elements: light, fish, sleep, the sinking of both the sun and the self, the lifeboat, and red to blue. This cosmos, which is extended somewhat in section four and becomes the powerful image of night in section five, has been dropped from "A Deathdream" completely.

While as readers we cannot complain about these exclusions in light of the brilliantly controlled unity of "A Deathdream," we can see that the wide range of imagery and the cosmoslike challenge of "Written Down in 1932" has been forfeited. The power of night and death and the problem of the author's positive-negative relationship to these elements has had to be sacrificed in order to obtain formal control.

The bird is expanded and given a greater role in "A Deathdream." Its diplomatic fight for freedom, the complex dichotomy between immobility and flight about which the bird seems to complain and which it represents, its clearer identity, give insight into the formal problem of dream versus ideal which Ekelöf is apparently trying to bring into his poetry. The petrified bird is suitable because it implies the possibility of flight, of escape from the narrator's smothered condition, yet keeps the bird within the sphere of stone; thus, it deprives the bird of reality and keeps it as idea, as a goal, or at least something different and possibly above the narrator. At the conclusion of "A Deathdream," however, the narrator is still lost, "Where am I? Wake up!"

These two poems constitute, to the best of my knowledge, the origins of "Voices." "Voices" itself, however, must stand on its own merits and my discussion is limited to what there is in the poem and what is associated directly with it. The title "Voices Under the Ground" gives some idea of what is to be expected. The most probable "voices" one might hear, or imagine hearing, under the ground are those of the dead. The image in the title also creates a concept of planes or levels. To suggest an "under" is to imply an "over" or above. Assuming the voices are coming from the dead, and given the title, the reader's first assumption is probably just that, the possibility is set up for a listener, for someone hearing the voices, presumably someone on the earth's surface.

Within the first stanza of the poem, there are two different styles, one that seems rather objective, and another that is subjective. The difference between the styles is emphasized by the indenting dash, often performing the function of quotation marks. The first style is that of the opening lines.

Common and simple sentence structure is used in the first three lines as typified by the use of the definite article in the first line and followed by the "It is . . ." of the next two lines. The lines, I suggest, are spoken from the most uninvolved level, by a narrator or the poet if one wishes to personify that level.

The next line, indented, is difficult to separate from the preceding lines, although it does seem less objective and the sentence structure is not as plain. The words imply someone who sees and evaluates, but someone other than the first person speakers of the following two lines. One theory could be that the first three lines represent thoughts of the narrator, while the next sentence may be spoken aloud by the same person.

With the two "I long from . . ." lines the first-person statement and vocabulary is almost colloquial. These two lines, it is presumed, represent the voices referred to in the title.

Basically, the two styles or tones within the poem are differentiated by third and first person speakers. Occasional passages are difficult to place, but these become clearer as our reading of the poem progresses. The first plane is that of the objective narrator or the stage-setter. It is this objective narration that may be considered upon or above the earth's surface, whereas the voices are beneath. This analogy will break down later, but it allows the reader to follow the poem somewhat more easily on a first reading.

Studying the poem from the viewpoint of levels or planes, decreases the importance of determining the identity and the number of the speakers. I find it easiest to read it as simply two voices in a dialogue, but since there is no clear way of verifying this, it may be read as a series of voices listening to one another and chiming in with comments.

After the stage is set by the narrator, the two voices continue in a dialectical question and answer method. For purposes of convenience, I shall label the first speaker, voice A, and the second, voice B.

If a generalization could be made from this point, the poem would be called essentially "associative" with a major portion forming a dialogue of the type presentday readers know as "absurd." It is distinctly a twentieth-century poem in that it lacks a traditional beginning and ending and presents a slice, rather than a complete picture, of a universe that lacks light, center, or surface.

A close reading of the poem is helpful to establish a basic foundation of agreement and to lead into a more precise idea than the generalizations above. After the two lines of longing at the conclusion of the first stanza, there is a long stanza that returns to the third person narrative and repeats in its final lines a resumé of the opening lines. It can be assumed, therefore, that we are back to the observing level of the narrator.

The contents of the lines reinforce this assumption, since they continue to fill the visual stage of the poem. The opening lines were abstract and not localized apart from the morning light and the floors of drugstores. In these lines the poem becomes populated. A young man, a pale girl, and additional details are added, such as the flowers in the window.

These concrete phenomena are left open to the reader's imagination and he is invited to use it: "she exists only in connection with her hand which exists only in connection with . . ." This invitation to the reader's imagination is extended by means of the bird. The association lies in the movement of the girl's hands and the bird's flight, and in posing the question of the relation or connection between one thing and another. The old woman and the man at the desk seem to be further details on what I refer to as the stage as well as examples of the problem of relationship.

No reason is given to connect these various singular entities, but the child at the blackboard reintroduces the question of relationship. Once again the association and the question are posed in terms of a hand apparently in motion, then of things related to the scene. The entire passage is summarized with "Where is the hand?" and with the references to the flowers, time, morning light and, finally, the black-white checkered floors.

The summary of this scene reminds the reader that a group of characters have been seen, almost as if they were on stage, but no plot, no reason to connect them have been given. Instead, the reader has been asked to consider what it is that unites them on this particular black and white stage.

Before we are given a chance to consider that scene, however, we are drawn into a conversation. The objectivity and narrative quality of the first section is dropped. "What a lovely name!" is a colloquial and evaluative phrase and the first person "My" of "My bird" verifies that we are overhearing a conversation. The two voices, who are familiar with each other, are discussing the extinct primeval bird— the archaeopteryx. The discussion at first has no apparent connection with the opening passage, but the references to flying and to light remind us of it.

A conversation about an extinct bird that is alive need not be illogical, if it is agreed that the voices actually are under the earth. Then an ageless sense of petrification, of time's progression in thousand-year beats is quite comprehensible. The voices identify with the stone of the earth and seem to feel an interchangeability between themselves and everything else that is within the stone. The dominant theme of the passage is the osmotic quality given to stone, envisioned possibly as a thick doughy substance or liquid, with the voice, lizards, birds, and presumably an infinity of dead life existing in it.

There is, however, a subtheme reminiscent of the opening passage. The concept of "connection" of "relation" continues by the absence-presence of the bird, and the same verb, flight, is used to pose the question. This theme of relation is further developed by creating a tension between the voice that is forced to remain "bound to the stone" and the bird "with its flight." Once it is created, this picture of voice, bird, stone, and their union, is broken.

One of the voices wanted to know something from the bird. We do not know what. The bird has the capacity to influence the speakers. "The bird took my wings and gave them to another light. The light went out." Although we do not know what the relation is between the bird and the speakers, we can see that the dialectical method of the poem is worked out more clearly here. The lines are reduced in length, and we can see a questioner and an answerer. Speaker A, the one who longs for the bird and who asked it for something, fears the emptiness and darkness of the pitlike abyss. Speaker B apparently delights in telling A of the confusing chaos that we begin to suspect is the universe. The description extends out to "the house of the stars," then back to the original area, "Birds and shellfish sleep there like you . . ."

The image of the stone is given even greater range. It becomes like a pulsing heart.

> With thousand-year beats beat the'r hearts of stone
> in veins of stone.
> For yearbillions of stone time swirls them with itself
> in raging storms of stone through seas of stone
> to heavens of stone . . .

The intensity of this experience becomes comparable to the pounding of one's heart during a nightmare. The imagery extends itself to the limits of the universe and then abruptly returns, apparently illogically to the speakers. A asks, almost as if he were awaking, "Where am I? Where are you?" B tells him to "Wake up!" The complexity of A's awakening is that there seems to be no difference between reality and nightmare. He repeats his earlier question, "Is there no forgetfulness in the house of the abyss?"

This question leads into a scene suggestive of a hospital and again is extended to a terrifying point of chaos. "Everything lies on its back, everything turns again and again on its back." Darkness is again a crucial aspect, and here, in the form of night, it becomes a frightening element climbing floor after floor of some unspecified building, possibly the hospital suggested earlier.

Speaker A abruptly takes us back to the black and white floors of the opening scene. The heart is now mentioned in the simile of the radiator, and the black and white floors are connected with the underlying "loneliness" theme of the absurd dialogue. With one more image filled with movement and implying chaos, "darkness rushes around the gables of the house," the opening scene is reestablished, with basically one character on stage: death.

Almost as a refrain the entire poem is summarized in the last four lines which give both the obejctive narrator and the two voices.

> Hours pass. Time passes by.
> Slowly the morning light pulverizes the drug of sleep.
> —I long from the black square to the white.
> —I long from the red thread to the blue.

Having completed a general summary of the poem, one remains somewhat vague and confused about the poem as a whole. Certain scenes are easily visualized, but to put the opening and closing sections into some kind of meaningful relationship with the central dialogue is difficult.

In an attempt at solidifying our understanding of the poem's structure, I shall briefly digress to some of Ekelöf's prose writings which are, I think, related to "Voices." During the same period as the poems of the volume *Late on the Earth* (1932), Ekelöf wrote an essay called "A night at the horizon." The essay, first published in 1947 in a collection of prose writing called *Excursions*, has since come to have a great deal of importance. In 1962 he authorized the republication of the volume *Late on the Earth* and stated that he considered it one of his major poetic accomplishments.[3] In the same 1962 volume he published a series of poems under the title, "A night at the horizon," and included in the supplementary collection of poems the essay originally written in the 1920s, which was first published in 1947, and now retitled, "Night—at the horizon."

There seems to be no doubt in Ekelöf's mind, and his evaluation has been critically accepted, that the 1962 edition does in fact represent recognition and extension of some of his major work. My concern with the essay lies in its opening two paragraphs.

> One evening in the dusk, at the close of the hour when cobwebs begin to fall, I sat at my desk bent over a chessgame which I played against my own solitude.
>
> Occupied by dividing my personality into an I and an opponent and concentrating in this way to reveal the secret cause of my deepest thoughts, I had forgotten the time and the room. On the chessboard which stood pushed aside in a corner, the chesspieces still defended a long neglected position which hour after hour had ceaselessly developed in my consciousness.[4]

The essential element in the quotation is the image of the chess game and the concept of the author playing against himself. The chessboard as an image is comparable to the black and white squares of the drugstore floor in "Voices." The concept of two selves, both of them part of the author, playing against each other is remarkably stimulating and, if effectively applied to "Voices," could provide a new insight into the speakers and the quality of the poem. Such a suggestion is risky, but there is one further piece of evidence that should be mentioned before the idea is applied to the poem itself.

In another essay published in the same book, "Modus-vivendi," Ekelöf combined the two images in just exactly the way I suggest they might work in "Voices."

> The scent of roast chestnuts: it is the wind on a street corner, leafless plane trees, rainclouds and gray weather, small restaurants with sawdust on the black-white checkered floors (which my thoughts want to play chess upon) . . .[5]

---

[3] Ekelöf, *Sent på Jorden med Appendix 1962 och En Natt Vid Horisonten* (Stockholm, 1962), pp. 169-171.

[4] Ekelöf, *Verklighetsflykt* (Stockholm, 1958), p. 137.

[5] Ekelöf, "Modus-vivendi 30-40 tal," *Verklighetsflykt*, p. 141.

This is a purely descriptive passage and it conveniently offers an exact combination of the floors that resemble a chessboard and the temptation they offer to the author whose mind seeks to oppose itself.

Returning to the opening lines of "Voices," several obvious correlations can be made between it (published in 1951) and the passage from "A night at the horizon" (supposedly written around 1933). Both passages begin with a reference to the passing of time, "One evening in the dusk, . . ." and "Hours pass. Time passes by. It is late or early . . ." The time referred to in both cases involves the subtle light of the change from day to night or night to day.

In "A night at the horizon" the author is playing his pensive chess-game. In "Voices," after the image of the morning light and the black and white checkered floors, there is the bitter but perhaps also pensive "tired as never years and days to death . . ." This line is immediately followed by a speaker, "I long from the black square to the white," who refers to the floors that resemble a chessboard. "I long from the red thread to the blue" is spoken by a second speaker. I suggest that it is the author's imaginary second self.

Let me refer to my initial introduction of these lines. I noted that the objectivity, traditional grammatical structure, and lack of colloquial language suggested a narrator, someone we might call an uninvolved perceiver. Now read this as the objective author whose thoughts appear in the next lines, "Silently, the morning light shrugs away the drug of sleep." Then he begins to play an intellectual game with himself. In the second essay referred to, "Modus-vivendi," he told us that he was doing this. Does it not seem possible that a number of years later he feels it unnecessary to tell us, but rather wants to show us the game?

A review of the poem along the above lines is useful at this point. It is easier to follow the poem if it is thought of as divided into levels or planes as I first suggested. A personification of those levels, however, would put the poet describing and thinking on one level, the outer or objective, and the two imaginary opponents on the second or inner level. Dividing the poem this way may seem a dubious method, but it can provide a fruitful way of looking at the themes and methods employed in the poem. The poet-narrator opens the poem. He describes, then thinks to himself, but as he sees the floor, he imagines his chess game, imagines he can hear the two speakers.

The poet pensively returns to an objective scene, but he keeps demanding of its elements some coherence or cogency that, apart from the passage of time, they do not have. The grammatical and syntactical differences, as I have noted, support this interpretation. The third person emphasis of "That young man" down to "with the black-white checkered floors" contrasts with the more human first person passages that precede and follow it. The observations of the third person are either critical, "there is something wrong with his face," unresolved, "which exists only in connection with . . . ," or questioning, such as the hand and the chalk.

If the two voices are in fact part of a fictitious inner dialogue, we should expect some carryover between the objective world of the poet and the conversation. This connection may be seen in the bird that flies "With its flight" in the observed passage, yet is extinct, made of stone, in the dialogue passage. There are other obvious similarities such as the verb "come back" and the essential questioning in both passages of the relation between things: what does the hand "exist in connection with," and what is the relation between the archaeopteryx and the speakers?

After this initial transition into the world below the black and white floors, the dialectic of the conversation becomes clearer. The transition itself must be seen as establishing the concept of time as a predominant theme. It was obvious in the objective world of the narrator, "Hours pass," and it is in the dialogue with its themes of extinction and petrification.

This "time" theme has ramifications that can be extended from my opening discussion of the poem. I suggested that the title automatically inferred an above and a below and quite possibly the living and the dead. This assumption is not necessarily discredited by interpreting the poem as occurring within the poet's consciousness. As he begins playing chess within his thoughts, he allows the central concerns of his mind to develop the patterns of the game.

The narrator begins with "time" and "connection" but allows his image, the black-white checkered floors, to influence him. He imagines a dialogue among the dead and continues his concern with the relation between meaning and time. If a bird above the earth is the symbol of freedom, as implied in the objective stage of the poem, then it is possible a bird would be the same symbol to the dead. An extinct bird makes the contrast explicit.

Through the image of the bird we are led into the debate of the two speakers. Their central problem is their inability to move, a fact more painful to them because "the bird is free." It can fly. Speaker A says, "I myself am bound to the stone, the primal stone." Oddly enough, from the earlier chirping of the bird and the fact that it cannot sleep, it is difficult for us to determine whether the bird can actually fly or simply represents flight. The clearest point is that the speaker identifies with stone, but would rather identify with the bird. The reason for this preference becomes clear in the next section beginning with "Is there no forgetfulness in the house of the abyss?"

The value of my suggestion that the voices are opposing voices within the poet himself becomes clearer in reference to this passage. Dialogues about the absurdity of the world and the universe are hardly original to this century, but this century has certainly overworked them. If the poem is simply an imagined conversation of the dead about the absurdity of the universe, it lacks originality and is somewhat confusing. If, however, it can be read not only at the above level, but at the level of the individual and his conscious and unconscious conflicts, the meaning of the poem is greatly expanded. The possibility of a "collective unconscious" becomes a major addition through such an interpretation.

The reason this extension occurs is that the narrator, that is, the individual human, becomes a sphere containing voices, dead and alive, just as the earth is such a sphere, and possibly the universe. Discussion of this sphere is the basis of the dialogue between the two speakers. Most of this dialogue can be studied as occurring either within the narrator or, in a more abstract fashion, simply in the universe.

The quality of the dialogue is reminiscent of what we find in absurd theater, yet it preceded *Waiting for Godot* (1952). Initially, A and B establish a surfaceless abyss in which lamps hold useless watch over stone. "This is hell! No, it is emptiness. And the house of the stars is empty . . ." represents a transition outward and away from the downward thrust of the previous part of the poem.

Previously, the bird was an ideal and the context of the poem was the earth or beneath. As the dialogue progresses, however, stone is retained but extended outward in a spiral of endless time. The emptiness of the universe is compared to stone, "For yearbillions of stone time swirls them with itself in raging storms of stone through seas of stone to heavens of stone." With these explicit lines the universe itself is envisioned as a petrified substance, an earth of rock rippling outward like circles in a pool. The effect of this image upon A is to put him to sleep, in a sense to hypnotize him into the spiral of stone. He is dazed and asks, "Where am I? Where are you?"

Speaker B wakes up A but their conversation immediately returns to the same subject, "the house of the abyss." Now, however, the imagery is centered upon scenes familiar to the average man. No longer is it beneath the earth nor in the sky, but almost at the level of the opening passage, a city building, where the two speakers discuss their world. The implied characters may have something to do with the opening characters. "And all these invalids who drift homeless around the rooms." The use of repetition and the apparent chaos of the scene combine qualities from the previous passages.

Light or its absence is once again crucial. "Is it night or day?" This night image is added to the city building and is seen flooding upward, again a motion reminiscent of the spiral. The passage openly poses the battle of light against dark.

> It throbs in the radiators like a strained heart,
> the lamps blink dead when they offer opposition
> and try to hold back the darkness.
> A white loneliness against a black loneliness.

The black and white lonelinesses refer to the floors and to the concept of a game or battle. The final lines of this section possibly represent the returning integration of the narrator's consciousness and the two players or voices he has imagined. The opening stage is once again present, but now only the man at the desk is there and we are told who he is: death.

The closing refrain concludes the cycle by beginning it again: the neutral passage of time, a sense of awakening, and from that awakening the admission or discovery of desire.

> Slowly the morning light pulverizes the drug of sleep.
> —I long from the black square to the white.
> —I long from the red thread to the blue.

My digression of tying the voices to the narrator and his vision of the black and white checks may be used now as an effective tool. The splitting of consciousness or, phrased in a different way, the process of listening to the voices within one's self, is not only a technical point but allows consideration of the themes of human consciousness and human existence in relation to time.

The narrator is listening to the voices of the past within himself. This means that just as time is a stonelike structure rippling eternally outward and enclosing layers of existence within it, so man too contains time within himself. The voices of the past argue inside of him. The substance of their argument concerns the meaning and quality of life. What is the relationship, if any, among things? Why is life chaotic and apparently homeless and futile? Is there any chance of escape by the flight of the bird, or by exchanging one location or one ideal for another?

The depth of these questions is strengthened by the technical quality of the device of the multiple self. As used in this poem, it is not unlike a Greek play with the narrator functioning as the probing and repeating Greek chorus. This repetition, association, and contrast may be studied to gain further insight into the poem. Ekelöf has stated some theories about poetry which are useful in looking at the structure of "Voices."

> Poetry to me is mysticism and music. Mysticism to me is not to nail together abstruse themes; it is the deep experience of life itself, the apprehension of the eternally elusive, shifting, returning in everything which is related to picture, tone, thought, feeling, and life.[6]

"Voices" seems to correspond to this theory of a shifting and elusive poetry. The two voices are preoccupied in some metaphorical or allegorical way with the continually changing yet related images of life. Ekelöf's mention of music provides a basis for further analysis.

> Thus poetry is for me an art form which has much to do with music because it occurs both for the poet and the reader, with words as notes, with the relations of word contents, with the nuances one word gives the next and the following throws back on the previous, like tone color, or harmony. . . . It is a form which among other things works with repetitions, motive repetitions, and

---

[6] Ekelöf, *Poeter om poesi* (Stockholm, 1947), p. 103.

development, allusion to what has been or will come, parallelisms, likenesses,
all of those devices in the power of which man seeks to "enjoy" existence . . .[7]

An analysis of a poem within musical terms is extremely difficult
if not impossible, but it may be fruitful to suggest the outline of a
musical structure within "Voices," since Ekelöf has indicated the af-
finity he sees between music and poetry. Such a discussion is obviously
indicative rather than definitive.

Even within musical terminology there are a variety of ways in
which a composition can be analyzed. I am going to employ a simple
structural discussion following more or less traditional lines within
the theory of harmony. This theory relies upon the concept of a
"key," a central tone or note upon which the composition builds.

Traditionally, the opening notes or chord of a piece of music establish
the key or tonic of the composition. This initial sound will be the one
that the ear refers to or orients toward as the music progresses. Thus,
the first passage in "Voices" may be called the tonic of the poem-com-
position. It centers objectively on time, "Hours pass," with light
and the two desires involving color changes as secondary elements.
The passage including the boy, the girl, the bird, the old woman, and
the others, may be called the melodic line in the tonic key. This note
or key is repeated, as it should be according to traditional musical
standards, at the end of the passage.

The second section begins with the archaeopteryx. In music the
composer is always faced with the necessity of making the transition
between his major theme in the tonic key and his most important
related theme, traditionally written five notes above the tonic in a
key called the dominant. One common method of making the transition
from the first or the tonic key to the fifth or dominant key is to play
some notes or chords in the fourth or subdominant. As I noted in
my thematic analysis, the archaeopteryx relates to the bird in the
beginning but is somehow not central to the following dialogue. Rather,
the extinct bird serves as a means of making just exactly the transition
described above from the tonic to the dominant.

The bird suits the term subdominant quite well because it leads elsewhere both literally and figuratively. Ekelöf devotes less than thirty

[7] *Ibid.*, p. 118.

lines to the bird itself, but he clearly needs and wants it between the objective passage and the dialogue. The tonic tone of time and light is kept in our minds ("thousand-year beats," "new light"), yet the bird dominates this section and allows us to progress comfortably into the dialogue of the speakers.

The speakers are important in the last section of the bird's subdominant section, but they come completely into their own with the line, "Is there no forgetfulness in the house of the abyss?" This line completes the transition to the dominant tone, a tone representing in this case the theme of the described chaos and its relation to the voices.*

This transition is indicated technically by the shorter question and answer lines. "Is there no light? Not when it is out." Once the dominant is fully established, the longer line returns, then leads back again to the choppier rhythm of the dialectic. ("And the house of the stars is empty" is the fuller and longer line. The short lines reappear in "Where am I? Where are you?")

From the "Where am I?" passage, we are in a final transition returning directly to the tonic. There is a repetition of the abyss theme and actual repetitions such as "Is there no forgetfulness in the house of the abyss?" A subtle nuance may be shown by noting the "Is it day or night?" in the progression from the subdominant to dominant. In the transition from dominant back to tonic, we read "Is it night or day?" It is difficult to conjecture about the meaning of such a change, but I suspect that it tends to emphasize "night" at this point of the poem whereas earlier the speaker had anticipated day. The absence of the bird from this transition is significant in itself; it almost admits the loss of the ideal.

If, as seems probable, the bird and its flight represent the hope for escape from man's condition, the direct return to the tonic from the dominant musically deletes that hope. The conclusion of the dominant section starts picking up notes from the tonic. The return to the city building leads back to the radiators, the black and white floor, and finally to the shadow at the desk. From the line "A white loneliness against a black loneliness," we are back to the tonic.

* (A colleague has suggested that this could be seen as a return to the tonic and thus the whole poem a development of, or theme and variation on, the tonic.)

The full tonic chord is repeated at the end of the poem in a carefully
reduced form. This return to the tonic is not only musically appropriate,
but fits in with the continuing theme of the voices within the poet,
the continuing temptation of his mind to play chess on the checkered
floor. The emphasis on death and darkness gives a pessimistic strength
to the closing tonic chord.

Reviewing my suggested musical structure, after the simple tonic
note of time is set, the subdominant bird leads the two voices first to
the bird itself, then to a wide open space that becomes the dominant
"abyss." Finally, the position of the two speakers within the context
of an almost universal abyss leads back to the tonic, to time. Death
serves as a deep tonic note several octaves below.

The question now must be asked: How does such an outline contribute
to understanding the poem? Can the intellectual or split-consciousness
interpretation of the poem be united with this loose musical structure?
Again, a quote from Ekelöf may be helpful in establishing how much
unity or order should be expected in his poetry.

> Order exists there [in the poem] only in a likeness, a not identical recurrence
> and if it also is open to me (say for practical reasons) to understand first the
> one, then the other as a central theme, I know that these themes are basically
> equal and similarly shifting and that it is the movement itself, the dance,
> which is really the main theme.[8]

Once more he emphasizes the musical properties of poetry and their
relation to dance or music. This corresponds to the shifting themes of
"Voices." Time's movement begins the poem; then the poet projects
himself and his experiences of time into the floor and thus into the
ground, allowing time to become stone, to become, figuratively speaking, "petrified." The bird's freedom is opposed to the limitations of the
characters in the opening section and to the voices in the dominant
section. The fact that the bird is extinct but can still be heard, and still
flies to give the narrator much "greater happiness" is a fascinating
addition.

By transforming his mental dialogue into the voices below the ground,
the narrator is capable of illustrating precisely how mortal limitations
are inescapable. The ideal is the only thing that is capable of flight

---

[8] *Ibid.*, p. 103.

above man's stonelike limitations, and even its flight may be only
"A diplomatic fight for freedom." In other words, the "much greater
happiness" offered by the bird may well be merely a gesture, almost
a tactful effort on the part of the bird to offer hope to the voices bound
to the stone. We note in both the opening scene and in this section
that various forms of "fly" and "flight" are repeated. No goal is suggested. The flight itself, the image of being above the earth, out
of the stone, is clearly what is important. The actual reality of
the bird, its real value, is discussed only in connection with man
and his limitations, as if the question of whether or not escape from
this condition is possible is unimportant in comparison to the importance of the *idea* of flight, the hope for freedom, the belief in
the ideal. "The bird says it flies away to give me a much greater happiness," says A. The reply of B, "A diplomatic fight for freedom,"
cynically suggests that the fight is not real and that it may well be
conducted, or merely stated, to keep alive the pathetic hope of A.
One could argue that the bird merely intensifies the sorrow of the voices,
since a few lines further on the bird is responsible for the extinguishing
of the light.

If human limitations and a dream of freedom are the opening themes
and conflict, the resolution is heard in the dominant section, the dialogue
about the abyss and night. It provides a further definition of the
limitations. Man's basic immobility is presented in the image of the
stone, and the chaos of the universe is presented in its extension. Within this universe man climbs plateau after plateau until he is destroyed.
The process is, of course, another way of looking at time, the basic
tonic theme.

Death's actual presence is not named until the poet has completed
his voyage from the initial drugstore to below the earth and to the
top of the universe. Then he returns to a city image, a building. The
conflict remains the same, light against darkness, man against time
and chaos. Death alone remains "through many generations of repainted surfaces."

How the various themes of time and man, ideal and chaos, play
back and forth is most clearly seen by viewing the composition musically. The intellectual chess game gives the poem human depth and
meaning, but does not make it the unity that the musical analysis

indicates it is. The shifting repetitions and varying themes within
the poem suit one of its essential questions: what is the relationship
between things? The musical quality of the poem implies that form
itself may be an answer. As will be noted when the poem's imagery
is analyzed, "form" is a word that cannot be easily dismissed or resolved
in Ekelöf's poetry.

Although his essay is extremely condensed, Göran Printz-Påhlson's
"The Scattered Limbs of the Poet" contains, I suspect, the seed of
much of what is going to be said about Gunnar Ekelöf. Printz-Påhlson
feels that much can be learned about Ekelöf's paradoxical nature by
studying the primitivism in his work. Printz-Påhlson points out that
this primitivism emphasizes man's alienation from modern society. He
then shows how crucial the dream is to Ekelöf. The dream fits into
primitivism as an instinct and, through Freud, as a means of reaching
the unconscious. Dreams have a strong metaphorical power for Ekelöf,
and he consistently uses them to discuss life, death, and reality.

Citing Gaston Bachelard's *L'Eau et les rêves*, Printz-Påhlson then
begins a crucial discussion of Ekelöf's imagery. Partially related to
Edmund Husserl's phenomenological studies, Bachelard has analyzed
the four elements, air, earth, fire, and water, in relation to the human
imagination. Bachelard's contention is that, while scientifically these
elements are no longer uniquely important, imaginatively they are
crucial because they are the essential elements, or areas of elements,
which affect the imagination. Bachelard's original stimulus was the
17th-century author Lessius who suggested conjunctions between the
four elements and the four humors. According to Lessius, the tendency
of each man is to dream about the element that corresponds to his
humor—the choleric man: fires, war, and so forth; the melancholic:
burials, graves, things of the earth; the phlegmatic: seas, ships, drown-
ings; and the sanguine: birds and things of the air. Printz-Påhlson
points out the obvious limitations of such a psychological approach,
but continues, "In any case it is easy to see that Gunnar Ekelöf is
both melancholic and concerns himself more with things that belong
to the earth, stones and such, than any other element."[9]

---

[9] Printz-Påhlson, *Solen i spegeln*, p. 104.

While Printz-Påhlson's criticism of Bachelard is legitimate, modern psychology has been able to move more securely in the realm between the poet, his poetry, and the imagery in that poetry. Charles Baudouin's traditional and representative work *Psychoanalysis and Aesthetics* has suggested that a cautious study of the relation between these three factors can add to an understanding of the poetry in some cases.

For a variety of reasons Ekelöf's imagery seems extremely susceptible to this kind of study. An effort to discuss the imagery of "Voices" within a psychological, and moderately psychoanalytical, framework seems justified in light of the fact that the poem may be occurring within the narrator's mind and at varying levels of consciousness. A general intellectual framework for the poem and a loose musical structure have been established, but if, as I have suggested, the poem is a daydreamed dialogue, there may be other elements that have not been touched.

I propose that the modern reader automatically begins interpreting the poem on a symbolic level once he gets to the two longing voices in the first stanza. The black and white, the red (blood, earth, Ariadne's red thread) and blue (sky, peace, ideal) have little apparent meaning unless they are interpreted symbolically. Baudouin discusses this sort of symbolism.

> The main characteristic common to the poet's imagination and to the dreamer's imagination may be expressed in a single word. Both the poet and the dreamer work constantly through "symbols." The symbol (in the sense previously defined—a result of condensations, displacements, and repressions) is the very essence of imaginative activity. It matters not whether the subject is or is not aware that he is thinking symbolically; the symbol is often the expression of the subject's unconscious.[10]

The point that Baudouin is making here can serve in two ways. First, it introduces the relation between the dreamer and the poet, and, second, it shows similarities between dreams and poetry which will be especially applicable to Ekelöf. Baudouin further explains this similarity.

> What we have to understand, when we speak of such a kinship, is that the play of the imagination is "identical" in the dream and the poem (to take the poem as a typical work of art). What we have to understand is that, properly

[10] Charles Baudouin, *Psychoanalysis and Aesthetics* (New York, 1924), p. 104.

speaking, "there is no such thing as aesthetic imagination or poetic imagination
—but simply imagination."[11]

If the assumption is made that the poet is the narrator, and in spite
of the risks of such an assumption it seems a legitimate and worthwhile
assumption to make, then the poet-narrator-dreamer introduces the
concept of the chessboard in the opening lines. The following lines
of longing may represent imaginary opponents created by the narrator
as he turns toward dreams and symbols. Bachelard describes a process
of turning toward dreams which I feel pertains to the narrator.

> Le caractère se confirme dans ces heures de solitude si favorable aux exploits
> imaginaires. Ces heures de totale solitude sont automatiquement des heures
> d'univers. L'être humain, qui quitte les hommes jusqu'au fond de ses rêveries,
> regard enfin les choses.[12]

The narrator in "Voices" is himself putting the emphasis on this
combination of sleep and imagination. One of the few lines that is
somewhat specific is "Silently, the morning light shrugs away the drug
of sleep." Few states are more prone to dream than that half-conscious
state of waking-up which the narrator suggests, and which the dis-
jointed imagery supports.

The next section introduces the various undefined characters. The
unfinished sentence, "That slowly morning light pulverizes the drug
of sleep . . . with the black-white checkered floors . . ." tends to create
the broken and confused state of mind that a sleeper or dreamer experiences.

It is important to remember Baudouin's statement that the process
of dreams naturally involves symbols. The content of the poem leads
to the assumption that the square, the lines, even the characters, and
clearly the bird are symbolic. The reason for their symbolism is best
understood in light of the state of revery of the narrator.

The black-white checked floor is the closing line of the second section.
The voices that we next hear are apparently those the title tells us are
under the ground. A further verification of their existence under the
ground is their identification with "stone," with birds and animals
that are extinct—buried under the ground. In *Love's Body* Norman

---

[11] *Ibid.*, p. 27.
[12] Gaston Bachelard, *La Terre et les rêveries de la volonté* (Paris, 1948), p. 10.

O. Brown, who while unique in some ways is still a representative Freudian critic, suggests that there is some significance to the fact that the dreamer suddenly imagines himself underground.

> The descent to the underworld is what happens to every human being when he goes to sleep.[13]
>
> The underworld cave is the cave of sleep and dreams; Aeneas comes back up by the gate of dreams. In the ancient world disturbed persons went, for a dream and a cure, to the cave of Trophonios; like paleolithic man. . . . The cave of dreams and the cave of the dead are the same cave. Ghosts are dreams, and dreams are ghosts: shades, umbrae. Sleep is regressive; in dreaming we return to dream time—the age of heroes and ancestors: Roheim's "Eternal Ones of the Dream," or the primal parents.[14]

If these statements are accepted as indicative, then the process that the narrator of "Voices" is undergoing is a return to a primitive state. This return or transition takes place by means of the bird; the undescribed and unexplained bird becomes a specific bird, the first bird to fly. I have already given internal reasons why the bird may represent the ideal, the ability to fly, to escape the stone. Brown verifies this meaning by illustrating the typical usage of the bird in literary contexts. He quotes Northrop Frye's *Fearful Symmetry*.

> The bird is not a higher form of imagination than we are, but its ability to fly symbolizes one, and men usually assign wings to what they visualize as superior forms of human existence. In this symbolism the corresponding image of nature would be neither the seed-bed of the plant nor the suckling mother of the mammal, but the egg, which has been used as a symbol of the physical universe from the most ancient times. . . . In Blake the firmament is the Mundane Shell, the indefinite circumference of the physical world through which the mind crashes on its winged ascent to reality. To the inexperienced eye the egg appears to be a geometrical stone, but the imagination within the egg soon demonstrates that it is something much more fragile.[15]

Instantly it can be seen how effectively this paragraph applies to the Ekelöf poem and how the problem that it poses, breaking through the shell, is a different metaphor for the problem facing the two voices. There is a similar analogy in Herman Hesse's *Demian* in which the

---

[13] Norman O. Brown, *Love's Body* (New York, 1966), p. 52.
[14] *Ibid.*, p. 46.
[15] *Ibid.*, p. 45.

bird must break through the egg of the world in order to fly to its mystical god.[16]

What I am attempting to establish by these outside quotes and references is that Ekelöf is working at what is called a "universal" level, that the experience the narrator describes and enacts is unique in terms of language and creation, but common (in a profound sense of that word) in terms of its structure and to some degree its imagery.

Brown discusses the dreamer in greater depth. For now, I am going to emphasize sleep and its imagery and say as little as possible about the sexual aspects of the references. The essential need is to show the relationship between the poet-narrator and the dreamer in "Voices."

> The womb into which the sleeper withdraws is at the same time his own body. The dreamer sinks into himself. And makes himself a whole new world; a manmade world, in the deepest sense. A whole new world out of the body of the dreamer, a world which is his cave.
>
> To make a world out of himself the dreamer must not only split with the world, self and environment, but also split himself into both self and world, self and environment, mother and child.[17]
>
> The split of self from environment, and of self into both self and environment, is also the split of self or soul from body. The essence of dreaming is duplication, division; as in schizophrenia.[18]

The withdrawal and split described by Brown corresponds to the process of "Voices." After the initial introduction of the tension between waking and sleeping, the splitting of the self from environment occurs through the series of questions about the figures, then the turn inward, the regression or introversion that leads to the doubling of the self.

---

[16] This is a point that I would have liked to follow up but could not. As the third chapter shows, I suggest similarities between Jung and Ekelöf. Hesse is also known to have been influenced by the psychology of his times and Theodore Ziolkowski in *The Novels of Herman Hesse* (Princeton, 1965) touches upon ties between Jung and Hesse. He quotes this passage from *Demian*. "The third is breaking its way out of the egg. The egg is the world. He who wishes to be born must destroy a world. The bird flies to god. The god is Abraxas (p. 111)." While one is tempted to relate this bird to the bird in "Voices," the "abraxas" reference may also be related to "Absentia Animi" and Jung himself has published a work on "abraxas," as Miguel Serrano mentions in his *C. G. Jung and Hermann Hesse* (London, 1966).

[17] Brown, *Love's Body*, p. 49.

[18] *Ibid.*, p. 51.

Maud Bodkin in *Archetypal Patterns in Poetry* emphasizes a very similar pattern that she relates to a poet's psychological "renewal of life" as suggested by C. G. Jung.[19] Exactly how her suggestion fits will be noted in chapter three. At present, all we need realize is that the rebirth does not occur.

The bird represents the attempt at breaking through the egg of the universe, the womb of the narrator's own limitations. The impossibility of that breakthrough, of attaining the freedom he seeks, leads into the next dialogue.

The central image for the entire dialogue is that of stone. The poet's decision to use the earth as the source of the voices is explicable in terms of content as I have indicated. Such an image, however, is rich with other implications that have been implied in the above quotations. Psychoanalysts would emphasize the relation between the womb and the cave, and then examine sexual connotations of the poem. Bachelard, however, emphasizes substance over form.

It is his claim that often the image and even more significantly the substance of an image created by the artist will affect further development of his imagery and his conceptual progression. In "Voices" it would seem ridiculous to analyze the earth or womb regression and to exclude the stone.

> Toute notre éducation littéraire se borne à cultiver l'imagination formelle, l'imagination claire. D'autre part, comme les rêves sont le plus souvent étudiées uniquement dans le développement de leurs formes, on ne se rend pas compte qu'ils sont surtout "une vie mimée de la matière," une vie fortement enracinée dans les éléments matériels. En particulier, avec la succession des formes, on n'a rien de ce qu'il faut pour mesurer la "dynamique" de la transformation. . . . On ne peut comprendre la dynamique du rêve si on la détache de la dynamique des éléments matériels que le rêve travaille.[20]

The advantage of looking at "Voices" from this viewpoint of "matter" or "substance," and the effect that substance has on content, is clear if it is realized how profound the idea of resistance is to the poem and how suitable the image of the earth and stone is to that idea. "La terre . . . a comme premier caractère une 'résistance.'"[21] Bachelard

---

[19] Maud Bodkin *Archetypal Patterns in Poetry* (London, 1951).
[20] Bachelard, *L'Eau et les rêves* (Paris, 1942), p. 176.
[21] Bachelard, *La Terre et les rêveries*, p. 10.

points out that the earth is the only one of the four elements which always requires a positive effort to manipulate. By using the word "stone," Ekelöf is projecting the field of the poem into the most severe and stringent of limitations known to man. Note how this contrasts with the traditional liquid warmth of the womb.

The opening lines of the "bird" section establish the major substance of the poem. If a sleepily perceived "time" was the only "substance" really tying the first section together, and it is difficult to find any other, the dominance of the stone that is established in the second section determines the major context, the predominant feeling of context for the entire poem.

The substance is presented powerfully. When Ekelöf writes, "I fondled it already as a stone," and talks of a heart, veins, and bird, the intensity of the paradox strikes the reader not only because there is a contrast between animate and inanimate, human and mineral, but because the substances themselves are strongly contrasted: the feather of a bird, the flesh and blood of a heart, stone.

This metaphor abruptly gives time a new force. Much of the power that comes from this union of time and stone is experienced by the reader at an almost subconscious level. Stone is traditionally associated with the beginning of time, a barren image of primordial creation, or simply the flat surface of a sterile space.

The substantial structure of the poem has been changed in even another way. Whereas the opening images were basically visual, the voices are audial with perhaps additional oppressive tactile associations. Thus, a variety of effects is produced upon the reader by the image of unidentified voices coming from the ground. Historically, there is the tradition of the oracles who interpreted noise or actual voices coming from the earth. In fantasy, one of the greatest fears is to be buried alive.

This new framework does not conflict with my previous explanations of the voices and the bird. But as the quotes from Baudouin and Brown have indicated, this transition to the underground and its element can be expected in dreams and daydreams. The narrator of the poem as he begins his dialogue with himself is extending what one might call dialectical tentacles that juxtapose the visual and the audial, air and stone, mobility and immobility, light and darkness and, ultimately, life and death.

The effect of the extreme range and multiplicity of these "tentacles" is to make each image stronger. The paradox of the bird's flight and nonflight is intensified, an effect that Ekelöf probably intended since the archaeopteryx is supposedly the first bird to have experienced the sensation of flight.[22]

The intensification of the concept of flight serves to give the stone greater weight, greater actual intensity. Its immobilizing properties become even more painful.

> I long for the bird which flies and flies
> with its flight.
> I myself am bound to the stone, the primal stone.

As this section of the poem continues, we get a clearer picture of the relation between the voices and the stone. Although they are made of stone, "I fondled a stone, I became a stone," and are theoretically surrounded by stone, they are mobile within it. For instance, the voices can "grope" around, and later in the poem they seem to have an ability to move vertically.

Where they are that they can move around in this world of stone is localized as "the house of the abyss." The paradox of this "house" of stone from which the voices can speak and move remains one of the questions yet to be answered. Previously, I attempted to establish the poem as a coherent structure representing a dreamer in some sort of dialogue with himself. I then tried to establish that this claim is consistent along both psychological and literary grounds. If the general structure is functioning along so-called universal lines, is the central image of the poem functioning at the same level?

The facts immediately obvious about the house of the abyss are: that it is the dwelling of the two voices and presumably a great many others; that its major component is approximately a liquid stone, and that it is dark. This description, apart from the dilemma of the liquidlike stone, could easily be an underground cave, grotto, or an underground labyrinth. Bachelard suggests that these are common locations in dreams. He separates caves and labyrinths. The lack of motion in terms of the

---

[22] Olof Lagercrantz, in a talk at the University of California, Berkeley, said that Ekelöf had read of the possibility that the archaeopteryx had been the first bird to fly and was fascinated by the idea.

two voices in the early part of the poem might indicate a cave under the ground. I am not suggesting there is a cave, as this seems to contradict the poem, but that there are associations that may be related to a cave.

> Ainsi, pour le rêveur de la grotte, la grotte est plus qu'un maison, c'est un être qui répond à notre être par la voix, par le regard, par un souffle. C'est aussi un univers.[23]

While this "living universe" may be related to Ekelöf's "house of the abyss," Bachelard gives examples of scholars who suggest that primitive man may have felt such caves to be reductions of the cosmos, and one who thinks that Plato's cave is based upon this concept. This fits in quite well with the poem as my study of it has developed so far. The lack of motion associated with the two voices, however, changes shortly after the "I groped around, got nothing in my hands" line.

We get the sensation of movement as "The earth winds, slowly and feelinglessly, time around its axis," and there is a concrete statement in "The feet must step on the stairs of the endlessly winding spiral staircase . . ." Since, according to Bachelard, the dreamer never realizes that he is in a labyrinth, this section may resemble a labyrinth. Bachelard discusses the differences between the cave and the labyrinth.

> En accentuant les différences, on peut dire que les images de la grotte relèvent de l'imagination du repos, tandis que les images du labyrinthe relèvent de l'imagination du mouvement difficile, du mouvement angoissant.[24]

I suggest that the voices resemble those first of the cavedreamer, then of the labyrinth, and finally at the conclusion the cave again. If this seems confusing, the most obvious comparison is in fact that of the womb. The embryo is enclosed in a cavelike sphere, yet surrounded by and almost part of its watery substance. Movement within such a dreamed situation could easily be related to the labyrinth discussed by Bachelard. Bachelard says of the cave.

> La grotte est une demeure. Voilà l'image la plus claire. Mais du fait même de l'appel des songes terrestres, cette demeure est à la fois la première demeure et la dernière demeure. Elle devient une image de la maternité, de la mort.[25]

---

[23] Bachelard, *La Terre et les rêveries du repos* (Paris, 1948), p. 202.
[24] *Ibid.*, p. 185.
[25] *Ibid.*, p. 213.

I do not want to study Ekelöf psychoanalytically, yet it is difficult to deny the womb quality of the particular image with which we are dealing. The essential point is that Bachelard's generalization, based upon his extensive reading, fits Ekelöf's poem, if we think back to my earlier readings of it. In addition, Bachelard adds the dimension of the regressive voices lost in a labyrinth.

> On a dit que dans l'homme "tout est chemin"; si l'on se réfère au plus loin-tain des archétypes, il faut ajouter: dans l'homme tout est chemin perdu. Attacher systématiquement le sentiment d'être perdu à tout cheminement inconscient, c'est retrouver l'archétype du labyrinthe. Marcher péniblement en rêve, c'est être perdu, c'est vivre le malheur de l'être perdu.[26]

Bachelard gives an example of a labyrinthian dream that corresponds remarkably well to "Voices." It includes a dreamer imagining himself swimming underground in stratified layers. The material is viscous, but there are all sorts of fossils within it. If we accept this section of "Voices" as reflecting by its archetypal imagery and structure that inner consciousness or unconsciousness that can be discovered in dreams and in poetry, this central section becomes profoundly meaningful. The often repeated "sleep" as well as "Wake up" and "Is it night or day?" suddenly fit within the context of the major part of the poem.

As the poem progresses, the language of someone asleep or dreaming and the imagery of the stone disappear. Why? Precisely because the transition already mentioned in the music section is occurring, which will bring the poem back to the surface and back to a level nearer to that of wakefulness. This progression is seen as the stone is expanded to the farthest possible point, "through seas of stone to heavens of stone. Where am I? Where are you? Wake up!"

This climactic stone passage, whether directly related to the speakers or indirectly to the narrator's dream, is a typical moment to cause the wakening process to begin. The stone imagery disappears and we are taken into a new kind of chaos where the major element is night, night rushing upward through the apartment building, a building one sees only on the earth's surface.

The awakening is barely observable. It is less an awakening than a return to the original state of the narrator. Night and black remain

[26] *Ibid.*, p. 213.

as predominant substances; their shapes as forms are weak, yet their power comes from their usage not as forms but as substances, as a black mass fighting against light, against life.

This final use of the image of night gives us a clearer understanding of the battle between life and death which is going on in the poem, a battle that is nearly unnoticeable in the first few readings.

> Pour un rêveur des voix souterraines, des voix étoufées et lointaines, l'oreille révèle des transcendances, tout un au-delà de ce qu'on peut toucher et voir. Et D. H. Lawrence a justement écrit (*Psychoanalysis and the Unconscious*): alors le sens de la nuit, et surtout le sens de la plus sensible des nuits: la nuit souterraine, nuit enclose, nuit de la profondeur, nuit de la mort.[27]

What is it that drives the narrator backward in time and inward to an uncomfortable and almost schizophrenic dialogue and journey within himself? The "longing" that begins and concludes the poem suggests some inherent dissatisfaction within the narrator. Stated simply, the voices seek throughout the poem to find a place that they can inhabit comfortably. They are continuously frustrated in this search. This concept of a refuge, of having a home or a space one can call one's own is common to both animals and men. Bachelard says, "all really inhabited space bears the essence of the notion of home."[28]

It is useful to recall that all the psychologists I have quoted, using very different techniques, have drawn a parallel between the sleeper's cave and the womb. I suggest, then, that the ultimate motive of the narrator, which leads him to reject the lack of connection or relation between things and to take the painful inner voyage that we essentially hear in the dialogue of the voices, is this need for refuge, for a sense of home. Notice how consistently this theme recurs in the imagery.

From the opening pulverization of the "drug of sleep" to the voices within the ground, there is a progression of such references: "the *house* of the abyss," fish swimming in water (their natural element), "the *house* of the stars," the flight of souls out of the universe and the repetition of "the house of the abyss." This theme is continued by "invalids who drift *homeless* around the rooms," and is concluded by

---

[27] *Ibid.*, p. 194.
[28] Bachelard, *The Poetics of Space*, trans. M. Jolas (New York, 1964), p. xi.

the flooding apartment building and "darkness rushes around the gables of the *house*."

The narrator expresses his discomfort by creating a universe of displaced figures, a universe extending from the almost primordial voices within himself to the stars and whatever life one may imagine in space. This intense need for a home may give one final insight into the poem. What is the value of dreaming for the narrator? Presumably, he cannot accept the lack of logic in the world around him and thus attempts to escape by dreaming. How is this need for a home, a refuge, related to the act of dreaming? Bachelard suggests one possible answer.

> if I were asked to name the chief benefit of the house, I should say: the house shelters daydreaming, the house protects the dreamer, the house allows one to dream in peace. . . . The values that belong to daydreaming mark humanity in its depth. Daydreaming has a privilege of autovalorization. It derives direct pleasure from its own being.[29]

Here is the potential of a mirrorlike phenomenon in which the narrator virtually dreams of a place to dream. Flaunted by his failure to find comfort even within his daydream, the narrator turns, perhaps must turn, to the final refuge, death. Death, "a useless caretaker," may take care of the only house left to the narrator. Facing this possibility, he hears the final echo of the longing within him. Ironically, the morning light chases away sleep, the source of dreams, and forces him to face the passage of time, and the frustration of his longing, thus, continuing the poem's circle.

> Hours pass. Time passes by.
> Slowly the morning light pulverizes the drug of sleep.
> —I long from the black square to the white.
> —I long from the red thread to the blue.

The complexity of "Voices," the control apparent in it, the depth of the dream process described, and the use of archetypal images, make it difficult to believe that the poem was not written in a single short and intense period. The poem nevertheless evolved over a period of twenty years. By reviewing the earlier poems, Ekelöf's long interest is seen in dream, in life and death, and in the need to find a space that he could comfortably inhabit, a home.

[29] *Ibid.*, p. 6.

"Written Down in 1932" shows more clearly than "Voices" the narrator's concern with animals in their natural elements, birds in the air, fish in the sea, and so forth. Saying first that he has "no refuge in sleep or truth my dreams are extinguished . . . ," the narrator leaves his own homelessness for a discussion of shellfish and fish apparently in water. The stone that he caresses or fondles becomes a home for petrified birds. These images are related to the narrator's inability to sleep and dream.

The narrator almost envies the sleeping shellfish and the fish that eat pearls in order to sleep. He loves sleep because it provides him with a chance to reach the sunken in himself, a place where he feels at home. Water is a traditional element of dreams and in the next section the narrator becomes more involved in sleep's drug and its loss. Light deprives him of the chance to dream just as the bird takes the narrator's wings and leaves him alone in darkness. Note the contrast between the bird's two homes, one—an unnatural one—in stone, and the other—his natural habitat—the air.

"Written Down in 1932" represents an accumulation of positive and negative reactions. The narrator, alienated from reality, seeks to dream, but the morning light deprives him of even that. His identification with stone is the next logical step, for the earth is the final home. There are a series of images in section three which support the paradox implied here.

Light and birds are traditionally positive, but here they deprive the narrator of his chance to dream. His identification with the petrified birds is in a sense establishing his own home within death. The dilemma, of course, is that he cannot dream there either. The fourth section continues the narrator's dilemma and alienation, "No lampdreams scatter the slum's need." Slums emphasize man's homelessness just as, in the fifth section, does the loss of identity.

It is appropriate that the last section centers around imagery of night and what seems to be a modern building. The building, pitted against night, is the city dweller's home. The narrator identifies with it as if he were inside of it, just as he was inside of the stone. But the throbbing in the radiators is still not a fire or a heart, it is night. Thus death and darkness become in this final section positive phenomena.

Life is negative, "Life divides and sorts. Life passes death by . . . ,"
while death can "mix everything light and energy to a uniform consistence." Death is a deserted love, a rejected outsider obviously
comparable to the narrator himself, for the narrator seeks the unity
that death offers and at the moment is or feels himself to be excluded
from both life and death.

From the very beginning of the poem, the narrator feels persecuted,
divided, "alone in the puzzle." To be at one both with himself and
possibly with others, the narrator must be free of individual characteristics, "trivial facts," for these are the very things that torment
him; and life, by individualizing, by selecting, is the source of his pain.
Death offers unity, "uniform consistence," virtually, a whole man or
a whole non-man, which is exactly what the narrator needs. Therefore,
the figure of death who offers everything positive is the one who is
rejected, and presumably, if the narrator were to receive the unity
and wholeness that death offers, he would no longer be the discontented
and sick person he is. The entire concluding section puts the dark
elements into one positive circle: night, water, blackness, and death,
a circle that is close to or may include the source of dreams, sleep.

This early poem includes a dream and refuge pattern not unlike
that of "Voices," but the earlier poem is less effective and less well
organized. "Written Down in 1932" gives, however, a strong motive
for accepting the importance of dreams to the narrator of "Voices."

"A Deathdream" substantiates this process of introversion in which
the narrator of the poem seeks through dreams an answer to his homelessness. The answer that he discovers is difficult to explain. The battle
essentially remains between the bird and stone, but the actual conclusion may be consciously ambiguous. Is it a dream of death or a
dying man's dream?

Bachelard suggests why this need to find a refuge may be so crucial.
The narrator of all three poems is seeking a framework in which he
may experience tranquillity. His inability to find such a refuge mo-
tivates the contradictory drives toward life and death within him.

And all the spaces of our past moments of solitude, the spaces in which
we have suffered from solitude, enjoyed, desired, and compromised solitude,
remain indelible within us, and precisely because the human being wants them
to remain so. He knows instinctively that this space identified with his soli-

tude is creative; that even when it is forever expunged from the present, when, henceforth, it is alien to all the promises of the future, even when we no longer have a garret, when the attic room is lost and gone, there remains the fact that we once loved a garret, once lived in an attic. We return to them in our night dreams. These retreats have the value of a shell. And when we reach the very depths of the labyrinths of sleep, when we attain to the regions of deep slumber, we may perhaps experience a type of repose that is pre-human, in this case, approaching the immemorial.[30]

This statement offers an insight into the loneliness, within these and many other poems by Ekelöf, which is both positive and negative, the introverted loneliness that fosters creativity. Ekelöf's primitivism may be related to this need for a place to dream. It makes the self-conscious statements of the young writer more comprehensible, as his dreams were the source of his writing. Without the dream, in night or day, he could become impotent, homeless, and powerless in the most total and terrifying sense to a writer.

There is an underlying theme in the poems of the need or the wish to provide one's own light. "The harsh stare" of external lamps may show us reality, but they provide no internal illumination. One cannot renounce life, but if one wishes to create, the dream must be preserved, even at the expense of external life. "A white loneliness against a black loneliness" applies to the dilemma of a poet of dreams. Ekelöf is such a poet and he fought the dilemma throughout much of his life. The study of the precise nature of this internal conflict between life and dream, its origins, and its effect on Ekelöf's writing is the subject of the next chapter.

[30] *Ibid.*, p. 10.

II. THE ALPHABET BETWEEN THE LETTERS

> "Is there no forgetfulness in the house
> of the abyss?"

"VOICES UNDER THE GROUND" represents Gunnar Ekelöf's attempt to portray, and in some sense resolve, his own sense of isolation and of man's general condition of alienation. The poem is merely one of many, but I feel it offers particular insight into Ekelöf's writing. This chapter continues to expand the themes and images from "Voices" by studying three pieces of prose written by Ekelöf. While the essays range from fiction to nonfiction and were written at different stages of the author's life, I shall treat them similarly since they all have closely related subject matter. The essays appear to be autobiographical, but their biographical fidelity is much less important than their consistent use of structural, psychological, imagistic, and thematic similarities, some of which I have identified in the preceding chapter.

Baudouin notes that such thematic and structural parallels often occur. He casts some light on the overtones of the relation between a poet and his poetry which is relevant to Ekelöf's own writing.

> A remarkable and important law is taking shape in this field of enquiry. We might name it "the law of the subjectivation of images"; this law appears to us to be the corollary of the law of condensation. We have constantly encountered it in the course of the present study, and we have seen that works which were apparently objective in conception tended towards the realisation, in symbolic form, of a subjective drama within the soul of the poet; such realisation may be involuntary and subconscious, but it is rendered all the more striking by this very fact.[1]

The concept of the "subjectivation of images" clarifies the particular drama in Ekelöf which leads him to have such a hostile view of reality and to feel sympathetic toward death. Ekelöf's writing reflects the conflicts and limitations of his childhood. Whether the appearance in his poetry of the images that represented those conflicts is a conscious act on the part of the poet, or whether they are unconscious repetitions

---

[1] Charles Baudouin, *Psychoanalysis and Aesthetics* (New York, 1924), p. 299.

is incidental to the fact that they actually exist in his writing. By understanding the nature of these symbolic images, their dramatic interaction in the poetry can be comprehended. Baudouin indicates how he interprets such symbols.

> In addition we must, in order to understand the artist's vision, penetrate into what might be termed his personal symbolism. . . . This symbolism is determined by certain conflicts, which ever since infancy have been associated with such images. By retracing the images to their source, we are enabled to discover the meaning of the obsessive symbols, which are so largely responsible for the peculiar characteristics of any poet's work.
>
> We must remember, however, that this symbolism is never stationary; on the contrary, it is in a constant state of flux.[2]

A study of the essays "A Photograph," "The Sunset," and "An Outsider's Way," allows some of Ekelöf's specific personal symbols to be defined and developed. The alienation and split identity found in "Voices" is discussed by Ekelöf in "An Outsider's Way," an essay written in first person about his own life and attitudes. At one point in the essay Ekelöf discusses men who are born into wealth.[3] This division between rich and poor is more than a mere financial split, for there are men who are born into want, "who will always have a feeling that something essential is lacking and a desire to get rid of everything unessential in order to more easily find that something."[4] He identifies with these few born into want and explains how, although he did not experience poverty and lack of education in traditional terms, he considers himself autodidactic and a member of this poverty group. He states, "My own childhood milieu was well-off but so far beyond the normal and so alien to life that there was plenty of room for my own kind of 'want.'"[5]

It is this theme of alienation which is also apparent in "Voices" and here, as Baudouin's theory suggests, the poet relates a theme from his mature poetry to his childhood. The clearest explanation and discussion of this alienation is given in the short essay "A Photograph" published in 1958 (see p. 128 for complete essay).

---

[2] *Ibid.*, p. 301.
[3] (Stockholm, 1958), *Verklighetsflykt* Gunnar Ekelöf p. 121.
[4] *Ibid.*, p. 121.
[5] *Ibid.*, p. 122.

"A Photograph" was published in a collection of essays that had for the most part been printed elsewhere. Only two essays in the book *Flight From Reality* were new and one, "A Photograph," was placed as the last essay in the volume. "A Photograph" portrays the relationship between the narrator and his father and it suggests the importance of the father-son relationship to the author's own writing and his sense of alienation from reality. I propose that the crucial outgrowths of this father-son relationship are: the preoccupations with death-in-life and meaninglessness, imagery concerned with voices and the gap between word and reality, descriptions of faces that are vacuous and distorted and, finally, an inability to feel at home because of the boy's displacement from his childhood home.

The basic structure of "A Photograph" is a progression from the photograph in front of the narrator to the scene within it, then to the father, and finally to the boy himself and the memories he has of his father as well as the effect they have had upon him. This "standing on the outside looking in" structure is similar to that of "Voices." In both cases a narrator projects himself into something and discusses it from there. This method is also employed in the essay "The Sunset." The point of view that is of interest in all three cases is a narrator who feels himself to be on the outside, but with a capacity and a need to look inward.

The narrator of "A Photograph" first describes the interior of the room, and only after he has very realistically portrayed the salon for the reader does he "populate" the photograph. While this again emphasizes the separation between the main figure and his environment, the effect of this narrative method is to pinpoint attention on the figure portrayed.

The objects surrounding the seated man are "silent witnesses." Since the description of the man begins ordinarily enough, it is not certain why the objects are defined this way, but once the face is reached, the reader realizes the particular and peculiar quality of a photograph in which pieces of furniture are "witnesses."

> But what gives the entire picture its unique life, or lack of life is the long taut oval face. The forehead is high, the eyebrows moderately protruding, the nose short and straight and the chin strong. The corners of the mouth are slanted down and the moustaches seem to hang down loosely. The eyes look

toward the photographer but there is no glance in them, or how shall I say it: they follow only mechanically and automatically the photographer's proceedings with his box, just as the eyes are accustomed to even if their owner is absent and far away in other thoughts. The person in the armchair, however, has no thoughts, or if he has some they are extraordinarily fragmentary and subhuman. Inside the high forehead he owns a swarming reef. Nature will think hereafter for him, if an abstraction such as "nature" can think, or if a coral reef can think. The expression on his face I cannot describe other than by exclusions. It is not a dead man's face, not a living man's either. It has nothing animalish, but if it has on the other side something human, it gives the human a kind of transparent impression. I nearly said that there was something gloomily vegetating in it, but of the gloom one cannot speak for the expression is far beyond that and all other emotions, and not of the vegetating for it is nearer something lifeless. It is in itself a work so far beyond that and all adjectives and attempts at descriptions that one finally has only the word terrible left. Anyway the face is not inhuman, but it forces one to revise his idea of what "terrible" is. It is the meaningless.[6]

The first thing to realize is that the narrator is describing his own father. The effort at remaining precise and clear, at not indicating any emotional reaction to the photograph that is so depressingly described, is seen in the apparent absence of evaluation, as if the narrator is looking back at the photograph as blankly as the eyes in it look at him.

Although the narrator seems to be indicating complete freedom from the figure described, the sheer intensity of the description betrays him somewhat. Once it is realized that the man is the narrator's father, it betrays him all the more. "Voices" has a figure that approximates the man in the photograph. The first description of the figure occurred in "Written Down in 1932." "Death was passed by whenever there were promotions. Death stayed sitting there like some wretched servant." The figure "sitting there" gives the reader a clue that "Death" and the father may be closely related.

The description of the faces further suggests the parallel between the two figures. "The caretaker at the desk (painted well-worn pine-grain). He has no eyes." Is not this another way of talking about their emptiness? Farther on in the poem, the invalids, apparently dead or in a state of semi-consciousness not unlike that of the figure in the photo, are described. "Everyone's eyes are blank and empty

[6] Ekelöf, "A Photograph," p. 128.

as windows, one does not see night or day . . ." The figure at the desk is the only one at the conclusion of "Voices," a "shadow at the painted-pine desk," a "useless caretaker," and it is remembered that this figure is death. This substantiates a tentative parallel between the narrator's father in "A Photograph" and the figure of death in "Voices."

In the references to "nature" and to the "coral reef" brain, even in the description of the photograph, there is a tendency on the part of the narrator to return to some state of primitive consciousness, or to deal with the problem of the unconscious within human beings. This role of the unconscious or subconscious forced upon the narrator by his father establishes the need for the narrator to define not only his father's life but his own life in terms that recognize and presumably accept both the conscious and unconscious aspects of their lives.

There are a series of overlapping connections between such words as "meaninglessness," "unconsciousness," and "death." This overlap relates to the theme of "death-in-life" which becomes such symbols as the voices under the ground and the bird in the stone. This becomes obvious in the description of the face in the photograph—it is neither dead nor alive, and the adjective that represents the face, "terrible," also becomes "meaningless." The essay ties these themes and images even more closely together by giving examples of the ways in which the boy experienced the visible reality of his unconscious or dead-in-life father. One such example is the following:

> There was one day, a spring day, when he was neither apathetic nor restless but somewhere between: for this reason he was dressed in overcoat and bowler, got his walking stick in hand, and was taken out for a promenade with a nurse on each side. This, combined with spring, seemed to me very grand and promising, and I followed behind in their wake. When the trio came to the corner of St. John's Street and Jutas Hill there was a little fidgeting, but not much. He absolutely wanted to take the steep stairway—they were wooden steps in those days—and the nurses were against it. He even tried to hit, a little lamely, with his walking stick against the small of their legs. But because his thoughts or impulses were never of long consequence he was not difficult to keep under control, and the nurses had plenty of time to exchange conversation about the little intermezzo while they were still walking. The older and more experienced nurse was of the opinion that previously, that is to say, "in life," he was accustomed to turning off just there, to walk that way, and that it

was "still there." This, that in his presence they undisturbedly discussed what habits he might have had "in life," made a deep impression on me.[7]

The boy's affection for his father, which is never explicitly stated, is implied in the words "grand and promising." It is felt that the boy seeks for any sign that will indicate his father's return to health. This hope is strong enough that he wants to go out with the trio and watch, implied, continue to watch, for signs of improvement. The boy's hopes are shattered by the two nurses and he points out precisely why. The two women talk of the man as if he were dead. In the pain and resentment that he feels, the incubation of two seeds is suspected: the first is the rejection of an external world and its cruel reality; the second is a need to escape that world and the suggestion of the means for that escape—the unconsciousness of the father, the something that still remains within the unknown part of his consciousness. For the boy this escape could be accomplished by looking within his own imagination, perhaps even seeking his own unconscious.

The insensitivity of the two nurses may have given the boy great pain, but it also gave him the form of the dilemma that he faced— death in life. How does one respond to it if it is personified in one's father? He tells the reader that he was appalled by the way they treated his father, yet the attitude of the essay consistently attempts to keep a distance, to portray the problems of the man in the photo without letting the narrator's own emotions show. It is probable, from the description of the death-in-life face, that the boy sometimes found it necessary to treat his father as a stranger, as a living dead man.

The union of the various contradicting elements that the boy experiences is solidified and completed in the death of the father at the conclusion of the essay. We do not know the age of the narrator, whereas it is implied in the scene with the nurses, but the effect of the funeral on the boy is immense. Again the narration lacks any reference to emotion, but the power of the scene and the power of the dead man is stated.

[7] *Ibid.*, p. 129.

When one sees a man long since undone become truly definitively undone, the contrast seems even greater, perhaps because the border has long been so wavering.[8]

The crucial meaning of that sentence comes from the word "contrast," for it relies upon the reader's ability to imagine the narrator's emotion when the father was within the wavering borders of life as opposed to the emotion of the narrator when he sees the dead body. The true power of the man is stated, however, for the reader in the last line. "He did not haunt long. But he still haunts."

The form that the father took in his haunting was not only in "useless caretaker" figures and in "blank and empty" eyes but also in the boy's alienation and in the symbols that he used to express and eventually dominate that alienation. The death-in-life quality, its relation to meaninglessness and to a blank and terrible face has been observed, but the narrator of the essay tells more. Voices, words, learning, and eventually the narrator's ability to understand a crucial symbolic piece of reality are all related to this painful childhood situation.

Accepting the importance of the father to the narrator, as exemplified in the scene with the nurses and in the conclusion of the essay, the father's direct influence in the narrator's description of the father's speech can be felt. It may be important to note that in this less than ten-page essay nearly two pages are taken up by the description of the face and the description of the voice. In fact, the scenes lack chronological continuity and seem to develop associatively from these characteristics of the father.

> During this time he stirred and dredged in a low voice, but in a discontented and disputatious fashion. There were no words, for it was rather unarticulated, but what one could clearly hear was the "intonation" of the sentences. The words had disappeared but the intonation had remained, and it could be modulated and modified in several ways. What I best recall is that brooding tone. The other room from the salon I just described was my room and it too looked out on the street. It had an inner door to the toilet and the bathroom which was a throughway with the main door to the bedroom corridor. On the toilet he would often sit for hours and mumble in the endless, long brooding rigamarole, sometimes in a rising tone like a self defense, sometimes in a sinking tone as if he tried to understand the intrigue behind the whole thing, or perhaps as if

8 *Ibid.*, p. 131.

he went through items in a ledger or discussed business. Since the toilet was placed right in front of my door, I could hear all this very well, but what I myself did I have forgotten. Perhaps I looked at picture books or played; perhaps I faltered and spelled already in the ABC book, for I had begun to read with a governess. Of that ABC book I remember clearly and precisely the reference "NOSE" where the word stood in capital and small printed letters and in script, illustrated with a clumsy picture of a dog's nose (without eyes, ears or the rest that properly belonged). What a dognose was I knew very well for I had had a beloved collie named Guerre, but I could never get any connection between those letters and that fragmentary picture: and that incomprehensibility has in some way coupled together in my memory with that muttering from the other side of the door.[9]

This passage cannot but help give the title of "Voices Under the Ground" another perspective. It suggests why the narrator of that poem might imagine voices from under the earth's surface, that is, the poet had heard this smothered muttering in his childhood. But while the first half of the quotation gives the possible origin of one of the poet's key symbols, the second half tells the effect of this voice upon the boy's childhood mentality. It establishes a link between the boy's use of words, his actual learning of them, and his *inability* to understand the connection between reality and words. Further, the structure of the scene is the same as that of "Voices" in that the narrator is apart from and trying to make sense of incoherent speech.

The inability to understand the world with which he is familiar represents a crux in the boy's consciousness. His father is not only a visual experience, a man of blank and terrifying eyes, but an audial experience tied to the very meaning of words and reality, "and that incomprehensibility has in some way coupled together in my memory with that muttering from the other side of the door." This might be called the "dognose" problem, for it identifies in its earliest form the problem from "Voices"—to what do things relate? The problem is specifically tied to the poet's ability to make a direct correlation between a word and an object, and, in essence, it challenges the traditional obvious meaning of words. This correlation between word, meaning, and reality, which in early years symbolizes the boy's alienation, becomes a means of overcoming life's meaninglessness by poetry.

[9] *Ibid.*, pp. 129-130.

This questioning of the relationship between knowledge and reality occurs in "Voices," and it may be worthwhile to digress briefly to "Voices" to show its presence. The first example is the simple question of relationship. The narrator in "Voices" first views the various characters and then ties them together by the question of the connections between them and each other or the rest of the world.

> That pale girl! (her hand is in the flowers at the window:
> she exists only in connection with her hand
> which exists only in connection with . . .)
> The bird that flies and flies. With its flight.

This is a simple form of the little boy listening to his father's voice and trying to understand the relationship between the word "dognose" and the mysterious picture—the relationship between things. The more complex version of the "dognose" problem is illustrated in the following lines:

> The child turned toward the blackboard, always turned to the blackboard.
> The pointers' screech. Where is the hand?
> It is in the flowers at the window.
> The smell of chalk. What does the smell of chalk tell us?

A contrast is implied here between what the chalk's writing says, at which the child is probably looking, and what the smell of the chalk says. This is again the opposition between the abstraction of words and the meaning of something physical and real. Since "dognose" and "smell of chalk" both relate to the nose, the reader wonders if there is not a subtle juxtaposition here between the conscious action of trying to read, to understand, and the unconscious perception or recognition of something real. The child's experience had defined for him a dog's nose, yet his intellectual or learned world could not define it for him as a word. Does the narrator of "Voices" suspect a similar problem?

The point of this digression is to give a brief idea of how the symbols of a literary drama may change, but that in many cases the form of the image or problem is retained in a new structure. This is directly related to Baudouin's "subjectivation of images." With Ekelöf, there is a continuing parallel between the sense of alienation or incomprehension, which the boy experiences along the word-meaning line such as

in "dognose," and the boy's involvement with the father. This parallel
may be seen in the "oracle" passage. It should be considered more
than accidental that two of the major scenes between father and son
concern the lack of meaning in words or books.

> From the library, between my room and the salon, I remember too how he
> used me as an oracle. He let me open up a bible or he opened it up himself
> and let me point. That he opened it himself seems most probable, because
> I still have that bible and it is only in Psalms that he made marginal markings
> and underlinings according to the oracle method. "Take sword and shield
> and stand up for me; draw forth the spear and stop my persecutors. Say to
> my soul, "I am your salvation." What sort of information he could get from
> that I do not know, but it probably verifies that all oracles are obscure. In
> the margin in pencil there is written: "11/9 1913 4-6 o'cl. (7 is crossed out)
> acc. to G.E."[10]

Although the narrator seems to be commenting on the scene as an
adult, some ideas can be gleaned from it about the boy. No doubt the
child wondered what it was he was pointing out, and often tried and
failed to understand these oracular scenes and statements. The problem
once again for the child was: how should he respond? The narrator
as adult is capable of evading an answer, but the child had to try and
put his own intelligence beside that of his father and, just as he had
to try and understand the incomprehensible speech of his father's
mumbling, come to some sort of conclusion. This conclusion affected
the rest of his life.

The problem was that the boy had to deal with several apparently
opposing levels of reality. It has been shown that he rejected the
evaluation of his father as far as the exterior world was concerned.
The scene with the nurses illustrates the boy's rejection of a negative
interpretation of his father. There is a scene where servants of the
household who have experienced religious "salvation" are described
as having spoken with him and found him healthy and happy. The
narrator dismisses this attitude as ignorance of the manic nature
of the father's illness. Without conjecturing too much, one may suspect
that the boy's own experience with his father would have prevented
him from accepting such external positive evaluations. The problem,
therefore, was how the boy came to terms with his own attitude about

[10] *Ibid.*, p. 130.

his father. I suggest that the only possible way was introversion, that is, leaving the physical for the internal world of thought and dream.

The dilemma was presented to the boy in even clearer terms than has been shown so far and it forced him into a profound sense of displacement. It is related to the general importance of the house and of my theme of inhabited space. We recall how well the narrator apparently knew each object in the photo and how easily he could describe the rooms and hallways. The relation between the boy's concern with home and the father is clarified just before the conclusion of the essay.

> Often he was sent away to one or another sanitorium or hospital but just as often he came home again, for the same piety which decided that he should eat with us at the breakfast table decided also that he was better off at home. I myself was often sent in turn to children's homes, where for that matter I was never materially uncomfortable. And besides, childhood is such that even the most rejected and pathetic one always has some light memories to offer, for it needs so little: a glade in the sun, unknown flowers and animals, the country, fun on a beach can quickly cover the stranger and the strangeness. But loneliness at night with all kinds of terrifying images and among strangers, yes, even in a children's home the longing for letters or a sign of life can give aches just as fully developed as in adults, perhaps more so, for the child has his own powerlessness drawn into it.[11]

This passage establishes that the boy was sent from home because of his father, whom he loved, as complicated as the emotion must have been, and that loneliness and terror grew from this interchange between father and son and home and institution. How could a boy who feels that it is "grand and promising" simply because his father is neither fidgety nor apathetic resent being sent away from home under such conditions? The reader can almost imagine the young boy thinking that possibly his father might get better, or that at least he is more comfortable at home.

But the result of this exile was the further development of the "stranger" within the boy. He was left even more to his own fantasy world and to the dilemma of his life: how could he want to be at home when that painful and confusing man, his father, was there wandering around

[11] *Ibid.*, p. 131.

mumbling? Conversely, how could he not want to be where he was most secure, where his memories were centered, where his life, as odd as it was, was housed in a familiar environment?

To add to the complex situation, there is no mention of the boy's mother in the essay, nor is there in any of the others that I am going to discuss. The only mother figure mentioned is the pilot's daughter whose death is narrated. This absence indicates that the father was given even greater importance. The only other being described in loving terms is the dog Guerre whose loss is also included.

This rather unique childhood displacement forced the boy to find out how he could make himself comfortable in the world, and since that comfort was essentially unattainable because of the living and the dead ghost of his father, the only comfort found had to be in his mind and imagination.

Intellectually, the boy must have understood the tragedy of his father. By reduction and by the process of years, the contrast of his innocent but knowing consciousness with his father's mature but ignorant unconsciousness could eventually have become symbolized, "A white loneliness against a black loneliness." While such a phrase is far too abstract to attempt to define precisely, its application to the loneliness of the young boy and the lonely isolation of the mad father does not seem altogether irrelevant.

The path of introversion and imagination had to be the boy's means of escape from the painful reality of his life, but the escape itself is defined by those things from which he escaped. In more precise terms, had the narrator totally escaped from the problems of his childhood, he would probably not have written the essay describing the photograph. We find, however, that the imagery relating to the father's presence in "A Photograph" is seen in other writing by Ekelöf. In "Voices," for instance, the face and eyes, the voice and its challenge to reality, and the need for a place to inhabit comfortably are similar to those in "A Photograph." As the conclusion of the essay states, the father still haunts long after his death.

I think that the sympathetic description of an attitude toward death in "Voices" may be related to a positive acceptance by Ekelöf of his own life and his father. This acceptance occurs by a subtle process of identification with the father which is hinted at in "Voices" and in "A Photograph," and is clearly described in two other essays. The first, "The Sunset," was written in Prague and published in 1935, then published in 1941 in a collection of essays entitled *Promenades*. The second, "An Outsider's Way," was published in *Excursions* in 1947.

There are two quotations in "The Sunset" which specifically concern the dilemma of the father and the process of identification. But since it is helpful to see how Ekelöf continues to utilize and to intertwine the themes and images that I have discussed in "Voices" and in "A Photograph," I shall discuss briefly the essay as it leads up to the selected quotations.

The complete title of the first essay is "The Sunset—From a Romantic's Notes." The narrator of the essay is never clearly identified and he tells us a story narrated by a completely unidentified man. The first narrator apparently stands on a mountain and imagines himself walking through the forest. He comes upon a group of men sitting on the beach and identifies them in no other way than to state that they are preparing to embark. (See p. 132 for the complete essay.)

This introductory structure parallels the others studied in Ekelöf. It involves a narrator's self-projection downward, possibly inward, and continues with his listening to a voice. The introduction also sets up a dreamlike situation as well as a vertical structure, since the speaker is on a height. It is a twilight or partially lit scene and the narrator's "goal is distant." There is an air of unreality in the opening section of the essay.

The dream quality is first introduced with "The evening around me is full of mirages," but becomes more imaginatively explicit in, "I climb slowly down the mountain, without moving." The trees are enchanted; the sea restlessly dreams, and, finally, as the narrator walks, or imagines he walks around a cape, he sees a fire in a cave.

He approaches the cave and sees the shadowy unidentified figures. One of the men in the group speaks and it is the description of his life, coming from a distant land, which composes the rest of the story. For the most part it is not so much his life as his attitude about life which is told. Essentially, his story goes in a dreamlike fashion from bitterness and futility to a rather positive concept of growth and stability. He is, at the conclusion, deciding what memories he should take with him as he embarks, apparently for his home or some sort of promised land.

The speaker on the beach is from a distant land, does not seem to be certain who he is or was, and wonders "have I dreamed the whole thing?" He answers himself, "dreams are also life's destiny." He continues his description and his questioning of life's transitions. He uses familiar imagery, the sea and stones.

> The storms help us forward in the direction toward it [expression of the irrevocable], but calms bury and delay us. The calm, that is death, the ink on man's foot; the tar he sticks in. Either death does not exist or it is nothing other than the great delay, the hell that stones live in for everything lives.
> I am afraid of stupidity and inertia. I do not want to be left behind.[12]

This imagery obviously corresponds to that of "Written Down in 1932" and "Voices." The reader wonders about the meaning of the "ink on man's foot" and "the desk flecked with ink" at which death sits in "Voices." The idea of a "dark spot" seems to have special significance for Ekelöf. The essay continues to use familiar thematic material by dicussing a refusal to believe in reality and an inability to feel at home. The image of a bird is used as a potential salvation. "Perhaps a bird shall be born from the fire and lift itself toward the other land where the sunset is the sunrise."[13] The bird resembles either the phoenix or the symbol of Abraxas which Ekelöf uses later. Here, its meaning is less ambiguous than in his later writing.

As he continues, the narrator criticizes his present life and makes a statement referring to death-in-life. "We are dead in ourselves and unborn in ourselves. It is in the past and the future that we live, in wish and in memory. . . ."[14] What these various references do is to verify that we are in true Ekelöf poetic territory, that the themes of alienation and death-in-life are consistent. The progression in the essay sets up a transition, however, and the change, which is a major one, is based upon the scene that follows:

> Much later, in one of the big cities, I was awakened one night by invisible voices. I tried to defend myself against them, tried vainly to convince them

[12] Ekelöf, "The Sunset," p. 133.
[13] *Ibid.,* p. 134.
[14] *Ibid.*

to leave me to my fate. Finally, I found myself in a state of peculiar excitement.

It was as if I had heard a once well-known language to which I had lost the key. They were friendly helpful voices which at any price seemed to want to warn me, to teach me something that could not be delayed. But it was so difficult for them to make themselves understood in their language. I had to strain my entire concentration in order to grasp specific words and sentences: "Upward to the west," where I came from. And then I seemed to see a desert of human-looking stones. It was "hell which neared the earth from the southeast where the plane curves." This plane would be transparent so that one could look down: I had been there and seen. . . . Or something in that style.

For several hours they talked around me; in other words, my memory was profoundly revitalized.

What an odd mood in the room! The high window crossings white against the darkness; the light which shone reticently in the night, and there, in the shimmering brass bed, she who always used to sleep while I watched. . . . Everything swayed around me. I thought I could see over the endless water surface. Sleep lay far off like a fogbank over a sea. The stars were eyes which looked at me—there were no real stars. And I myself sat as awake as the radioman on some disabled steamer: as if everything depended on me. The whole time a swarm of voices and farthest away one lone voice that sought to reach me, that fought to make itself heard. It was as if against my will I was forced to hear incorrectly—as if another I of myself had forbidden me to hear.[15]

Quite obviously, in an only slightly more complicated form, the Ekelöf voices are seen here. They wake the narrator out of sleep, thus putting the scene close to a level of dream. It occurs in a big city and at first he resists the voices, then he begins explaining and describing them.

The "well-known language to which [he] had lost the key" clearly fits into the incomprehensible language of the narrator's father in "A Photograph." The important addition is that the voices are friendly. They are trying to teach him something, "but it was so difficult for them to make themselves understood in their language." If Ekelöf is accepted as the narrator, could there be a better indication of the underlying hope for contact between father and son? The son must have sat in his room listening to the voice (and here it is friendly), and attempting to understand what it was that the voice was trying

15 *Ibid.*

to say, perhaps even to teach him. We recall that the boy's actual learning processes were influenced by the voice; his ability to reject and to accept reality was developed within its sound.

In a later scene in "The Sunset," the narrator writes of his father, "the clear moments were so rare."[16] This means that sometimes the father was an intelligent human being. Biographically, it is known that Gunnar Ekelöf's father was a highly successful businessman and earned the family fortune before the breakdown that lead to his eventual insanity. This makes the boy's hope in "A Photograph" all the more poignant and painful. If the father was always mentally ill, the process of love and identification would have been more difficult for the boy, but if there actually were "clear moments" there is reason to admit that the boy could have psychologically identified with his father.

The passage from "The Sunset" enacts Ekelöf's own dilemma in a new form. The narrator is straining to understand the voices. As he fails to get any comprehensible meaning from them, he sees, "a desert of human-looking stones." This is the most painful death-in-life image Ekelöf can conceive, for the stones are hell. The image must be related to the narrator's attempt at understanding the voices and at having his attempt frustrated. The scene is tied even more directly with the father.

"The whole time a swarm of voices and farthest away one lone voice that sought to reach me . . ." The father in this situation becomes a kind of savior. The incomprehensibility of the voice leads to the concept of the split self within the narrator, one wanting to hear and understand, the other forbidding it, perhaps because of the pain associated with it. The split fits with the man who plays chess against himself in his own thoughts and who, as I have suggested, does it by hearing, by creating juxtaposed voices.

The major point of this scene from "The Sunset," as far as this study is concerned, is the narrator's implied admission of his affection for his father, of his childhood belief that the voice was trying to help him and teach him if he could understand it. This allows for a process of identification with the father. As this identification process develops, we realize that Ekelöf's apparent preference for the borderline of

16 *Ibid.*, p. 137.

consciousness, his primitivism, his combination of absurdity and mysticism, and his positive-negative attitude toward death, as he expresses it in his writing, may be related, at least to some extent, to the father-son relationship.

The father's identity to the son was even more crucial if there really was no effective mother figure in his early years. Before the next scene in "The Sunset," which exactly parallels the one I have just quoted, there are a number of scenes that deal with women. These scenes allow a differentiation between the childhood and the puberty of the narrator of the two stories, and they contribute to an understanding of the symbols with which this study is concerned.

One of these scenes again seems like a dream and possibly represents a period during which the narrator hoped that a woman or women could help him to escape from the problematic world of his consciousness.

> Then I noticed that I walked arm in arm with someone but it was as if we had not really been awakened, neither she nor I, as if we still dreamed.
>
> We went arm in arm in a gigantic room. It was a museum, but the walls rose completely empty. There was nothing other than a shadow-like immense stranger, continually the same. The room was filled with a gray green twilight, curiously translucent. One could see how he streamed around like the circulation of blood, inescapable and always counter-clockwise. And we two who walked clockwise met him continuously anew. Then he stretched his terrible, expressionless, threatening face toward us, always the same, quite near. . . .
>
> I pressed closer to her side in fear. I did not want to lose her—and anyway I lost her. At the exit I was alone, I do not know how. . . . I was alone in the purple desert where there was no human besides myself. The purple desert was blood-red as the sunset.[17]

Reidar Ekner suggests that this scene is a dream and that Ekelöf may have consciously given it psychoanalytic connotations when he wrote it. Ekner's interpretation of the scene fits with his study of the overall importance of the womb and womb imagery in Ekelöf.

> There is hardly any doubt about how the dream in general should be interpreted, that it deals with the yet unborn child's connection with the mother in the womb. The stranger with the threatening face, who moves in the opposite direction from them, cannot easily be anyone other than the child's

[17] *Ibid.*, p. 135.

father. At the exit, that is to say at the opening of the womb and in the moment of birth, the complete unity between mother and child is broken and the child is left alone.[18]

In terms of the story itself, this scene occurs among a number of scenes in which women are seen as positive figures. Apart from the psychoanalytic interpretation of this and other scenes, one feels that the narrator is turning to "woman" to save him at least from loneliness. That the stranger, however, is the father seems undeniable as I have reached the same conclusion as Ekner by a completely different technique. The word "terrible," the counterclockwise motion, and the expressionless face all point to the obsessive image of the father. Since the couple going arm in arm continuously meet the figure again and again, he suits the father who "still haunts" as he was described in "A Photograph." Equally important in this scene is the fact that the woman is treated not only as a place of introversion, but as a partner. This clearly fits into the Oedipal tradition, yet it touches upon the subtle role that women play in this essay.

The unique quality about the scene, and the reason it is a suitable example of the narrator's process of identification with his father, is that it allows us to learn more about the positive-negative attitude of the narrator toward his father. The voices that the narrator heard only two paragraphs above this scene were "friendly, helpful voices." This face is "threatening" and "terrible."

What the division between face and voice, between sight and sound suggests is that the death figure, "he has no eyes," can be the terrifying side of the father, while the voices can be the helpful, the tutorial. The face, the physical visual reality, of the father must have been the negative and fearful image of the dilemma for the boy. He mentions how his father ate eggs in such a disgusting fashion. But when the boy was not forced to look at this reality, this terrifying visual presence, and when he could only hear him, then his imagination was allowed to function. He could hope that there was some hidden meaning in the words, if only he could understand them.

Returning to the women in "The Sunset," there are several indications of the narrator's hope in them. The most beautiful portrayal

[18] Reidar Ekner, *I den havandes liv* (Stockholm, 1967), p. 84.

of this hope is the scene with the fisherman's daughter when the narrator is a young boy. A woman eventually comes to destroy his various pastoral visions, however, and at the same time she gives us a new insight into "Voices."

"But around the corner slyly smiling sneaked the old woman who stole children."[19] This is the woman who "sneaks and sneaks" in "Voices." We realize now what a threatening character she is in that poem. In this essay she brings the narrator's fears back and returns him to his solitude, to his estrangement and the motive for it. Given the lack of a mention of a mother figure and the association of this "old woman" line with the one that follows it obviously referring to the father, one wonders if this is not a negative image of a mother. Is this sly old woman a disguised reference to the boy's mother who "stole" him from his own house, who forced him to leave his home because of a father whom he both loved and feared? The line is followed by this passage.

> Why should the stranger always pursue me: why did I never get home? The well-known door. I knew where it was, but someone or something hindered me and held me back . . .
> And why did all the roads lead me so far from myself.[20]

These lines bring together the stranger and the home—the father in the home. It also suggests that the resolution of the narrator's problems will occur when he is capable of going home, of meeting the dilemma of the stranger and overcoming it. The narrator, for a few moments, then longs for the idyllic periods of his childhood, on a beach with a young girl, in a forest, but he returns to this theme of home.

> The years went by. One time I went home. The well-known door opened and I went into the little room with my eyes looking down to the floor. There he sat, the stranger, the sick man. His face shone joyfully when he saw me. Rays of sun played in the room.
> —Hello little grandpa, he said. Grandpa is here, hello little grandpa; come here little grandpa. . .
> He moved a little in his chair, smiled a light and bewildered smile. The nurse smiled too but coldly and habitually. Both their smiles were equally strange. Her stepmotherly guarding motions when she straightened the

---

[19] Ekelöf, "The Sunset," p. 137.
[20] *Ibid.*

blanket embarassed me and made me sad. One could not show that one was sad in front of the stranger.

Outside the bells boomed. The sunset glowed in the window. A last ray fell in the room, played on the wall. What should I say and do? "He called me 'grandpa.'" I thumbed my cap.

The clear moments were so rare. Otherwise he was usually far away. His face had an absent and decayed expression and his lips mumbled continually incomprehensible words which he got from far away.

—He hears voices, they said to me, and I understood. I did not know that it was only a manner of speaking.

For years he was as someone whom one has already said goodbye to, someone one recently has been separated from and who goes his way and whose face becomes more and more indistinct, soon a disappearing memory.

And the years went by. I lived as before under the peal of the heavy bells. They woke me often in the mornings. It was like waking out of a deep and funereal dream. They pursued me long into the mournful winter twilight. It was always someone who died so that they could ring.

Sometimes doubt came and grabbed me by the hair. I knotted my hands but did not stamp on the floor, only became more alone. No one understood me—it was a common complaint but I had an honest reason: I did not understand myself.[21]

This entire quotation substantiates the alienation of the boy. This is the first time that the voice, the face, and the stranger all actually have tied into the father-image. This unites poetic imagery and psychological origin in a single work and strengthens the probability of the union between the two.

There is a continuing degree of identification with the father. Although the face, the "stranger" distracts the narrator, he accepts the statement, "he hears voices," quickly, as if the narrator himself also "hears voices." We know in fact that he has heard them in the city scene that occurs before his return to his home. Eventually, the narrator will be shown more fully identifying with "the stranger," but it is useful here to recall that the narrator of "Voices" hears voices in a fashion not unlike that of the father in this scene.

The major elements in the scene are those that give other poetic symbols, which often reappear in the poet's work and are here directly related to the home and the father. It is my opinion that while Ekelöf was alienated from reality by his father, he also identified with him

[21] *Ibid.*, pp. 137-138.

to a limited extent, and that ultimately the poet used symbols of his
identification with his father in order to transform his painful world
into an artistic one.

In the above quotations, the "bells boomed" and the "sunset glowed"
while the narrator watches and listens to the "stranger." Later, he
says, "I lived as before under the peal of the heavy bells." "They
pursued me long into the mournful winter twilight." The bells and
the sunset are symbols that later take on characteristics of or are
related to the father and to memories from Ekelöf's childhood.

The precise way in which the poet used these symbols to transform
his past into artistic productivity is suggested in the conclusion of
"The Sunset" and explicitly stated in "An Outsider's Way." Later
paragraphs of "The Sunset" tie together the booming bells and the
father, and the narrator interprets the bells symbolically. He relates
them to his own life, to sleep, and to death.

> I remember how I used to open the window secretly and climb up the chimney
> steps to the ridge of the roof. The city lay beneath me and the sunset bled over
> the farthest roofs. All the city's bells tolled funerals across the world and I
> myself was filled with that most sorrowful music.
>
> To fly in the sunset. Melancholy blood-red was my color since childhood
> and I wallowed in the thought that everyone was going to die and I would
> be left alone in the world. What an opportunity to be finally completely
> drowned in sweet self pity. Or too I imagined that I died, lamented, and
> returned to the distant land. The roof lifted and swayed. I fluttered my wings.
> But I did not want to fall down. I wanted to fly into the sunset and burn there.
> For a long time it was like flying into the past, to bury myself in sorrow's
> beautiful blood-red earth.[22]

The bells are a positive part of the identification with the father;
they are audial. Nevertheless, they are used in this quotation in terms
of sorrow and pathos, but they seem to be heading in the direction
of an all-inclusive mysticism. The sorrow of the sunset and the bells
may easily be related to the pain-filled house and its pathetic inhabitant.
The flight, the bird reference, is a result of the need to escape from
the reality of the father, but positive elements of the father are included in the fantasy. Music and sorrow become elevated to an almost
therapeutic position. What is occurring is a young man adapting

[22] *Ibid.*, p. 138.

himself to the terms of his childhood and making the elements that
open up his imagination into a positive part of his consciousness.

This union continues in the next two paragraphs and it is here that
the reconciliation and identification with the father image occurs, not only in symbolic form but in what seems to be a conscious overt statement.

> The years went and the bells silenced one by one. I stared into the sunset
> with my entire soul. My attention became soundless. The star was lit in
> silence, shining nearly unnoticeably over the desert. And like an echo nearly
> inaudible an endless music reached me.
>
> Since then I have listened to the music from many heights and beaches.
> I have gone through darknesses. Half-blind and nearly unconscious I have
> beaten my way forward, to the west.[23]

The opening lines of this scene take those symbols closely related
to the father, the church bells, and the sunset, and transform them.
They become music and a star. This music is a new and more satisfactory replacement of the bells. The narrator's escape from painful
reality into the sunset is successful. The degree of identification with
the father is modulated to just the right degree of consciousness and
unconsciousness. The hearing faculty is given greater credence; he
has "listened to the music from many heights and beaches." The
borderline between madness and sanity is accurately reproduced, for
the narrator describes himself in these terms, "*half-blind* and *nearly
unconscious* I have beaten my way forward, to the west."

The narrator's feeling of success comes from the momentary feeling
of progress, but it is recognized that subconsciously the success is far
more important to him because he makes it within the exact framework
of his partial identification with his father. Verification of this transition may be seen by remembering the "voices" earlier in the essay
reaching out to him, trying to help him, telling him "Upward to the
west." In other words, the narrator is successfully following what he
could understand of the voices, the command to go west, toward the
setting sun, *home*, and those voices, the voice, is directly related
to the mumbling incoherent father. The narrator himself now partially
resembles the empty-eyed, unconscious father, and the resemblance is
a happy event.

[23] *Ibid.*

It must be accepted that Ekelöf wrote "The Sunset" with some degree of conscious artistic control. He was aware of the parallels he drew between the voices and the face. The sunset is not only the title of the story, it is the theme in the sense that it is profoundly related to his father. Recall how conscious of the sunset the narrator is when he visits the stranger. In the beginning of the essay, there is a blood-red sunset, and the narrator is isolated. After the narrator has visited the stranger and, as realized at the conclusion, comes to terms with the positive and negative elements of his father, he says, "Blood-red is no longer my color." This means, I believe, that he has overcome the negative aspects of his obsession with his father, such as the sunset, and is ready to embark for the future.

This transition is repeated in "An Outsider's Way" in almost exactly the same terms, yet with further indication of how he used the complexity of his childhood as a means of becoming an artist. Biographically, it seems probable, according to my interpretation of these essays, that somewhere between 1928 and 1935 Ekelöf went through a crisis that allowed him to transcend the dilemma of his childhood and to use images from his past as a part of his developing art.

Ekelöf's need to become an artist may be related to his childhood. The difficulties in his home could have forced him inward and the conflicts enacted psychologically could have become fatal unless they found an outlet. In "The Sunset" the need for an outlet was making itself felt in the boy's experiences on the roof. The first hints of a way of bringing about a resolution to that need are those relating the father and the sunset to music.

The concluding section of this chapter is devoted to the transformation of the obsessed boy into the potential young artist. The first emphasis of this transformation falls upon music because, if Ekelöf's writing is to be believed, the first stages of the transition occurred through music. The aesthetic need finally found its way to poetry and began its lifetime work there. It is possible that this eventual turning to poetry may have been a psychological necessity caused by the specific dilemma of the "dognose" problem, the relationship of reality to word. But the first step, as seen in "The Sunset," was a displacement of the funereal music associated with the father, to a more positive if imagined music.

This transformation is discussed both in its literary and musical forms in the autobiographical essay "An Outsider's Way." The essay begins with the poet's quotation on " want" which I mentioned earlier. It continues with the various brief adventures that led to Ekelöf's decision to become a poet. He says at one point, "My story is a story of boats not taken and trains missed."[24] What he is referring to is a series of decisions to leave Sweden and live elsewhere. Several times he did manage to leave Sweden, but he always returned. The goals of India and Kenya represented fantasies of escape, and although he did not succeed in attaining them, he did find himself as an artist.

He speaks of a trip to London to learn Oriental languages and of his return to Uppsala. There he wrote his first poems, significantly enough in a secret language that no one could understand. This is but another example of his probable unconscious imitation of his father. Subsequently, however, he decided to become a musician, and after practicing eight to ten hours a day one summer, he left for Paris to study music.

Before telling of these adventures, he discusses music and how important it was to his childhood. We have seen Ekelöf binding tightly together his fantasy of escape and his vision of the sunset. The music that he heard, in some mysterious way a replacement of the tolling bells, became a way of uniting fantasy and vision. In the following quotations from "An Outsider's Way," the same images and themes are combined, now directly related in the first person to Ekelöf's own life, and in the framework necessary for the transition to art—beauty.

The first quotation shows him as a sensitive child responding to music in the psychological pattern of fear and alienation which was predominant in his childhood.

> Music has given me the most and the best. The first time I heard a real string orchestra was sometime in the last year of the first World War with my guardian at a big movie theater, the Red Barn I believe. The "sorrowful" music made such an impression on me that for a long time in a kind of fear I refused to go again when I had the chance. The music forced me to imagine the most terrifying things: that I was completely alone in life, kidnapped or lost and had no place to go—it was an inexperienced ear's naive reaction in an

[24] Ekelöf, *Promenader och Utflykter* (Stockholm, 1963), p. 173.

age when one involuntarily objectifies all strong feelings, in some way explains them to one's self, exemplifies them, furnishes them with a written plot.[25]

The written plot with which he furnished himself was the type of fearful thing easily related to his father, the fear of isolation, of being an orphan. Is the word "sorrowful" in quotations to emphasize the war only, or is it as well an indication of the unconscious connection between the father and the music?

This next quotation apparently refers to a later period in his life. It makes the connections that will eventually lead him to view art as a means of responding to life.

> One of these characteristically strong early memories was the sunset. It fits, you know, for a young poet, but I do not know how I came to be a cloud watcher. The sunset laid heavily over my childhood and I even saw it in my dreams. The intense brick red church outside the window—it was St. John's church in Stockholm—cast a hectic, sickly and seemingly magnified reflection of the sunset deep into the room. In this red twilight my father wandered around like a shadow, mentally ill for several years already, mumbling with a vacuous distorted face, followed by the nurses. When they got him seated in an armchair he could sit for hours and hear voices, as it was called, which is to say that monotonously he mumbled and brooded, incomprehensibly and without finishing. It was an apartment with long corridors and in the twilight evenings a peculiar ghostly atmosphere ruled the recesses while the funeral bells rang outside. In my memory red sunsets and bells are inseparable.
>
> Later with the daring of my wilder years, I began to climb up on the roof in order to see the sun go down. The roof was one of the highest in St. John's Heights. I went up through the attic door and scrambled further, partially with and partially without the help of the fire escape, until I sat astride the ridge of the roof, where I smoked forbidden cigarettes and stared in the sun like an anchorite. The height was dizzying, the house's own plus the roof's, for the gable stood and swayed near the edge of an abyss, the bottom of which was our backyard down on Tegner Street. Beneath me lay the whole city and now and then there were glimmers far away in the windows of the castle, which were, perhaps, just washed by equally daring servants during the big autumn cleaning.
>
> I did not do it to prove I was clever—for that matter no one knew about it. But I was saturated with a fantastic thirst for beauty and completely incapable of expressing it. I do not understand how I dared. Sometimes I have terrifying dreams of dizziness.

[25] *Ibid.*, p. 166.

> The sunset climbing was united with musical extravagancies. I used to
> spread myself out in endless series of disconnected and often very dissonant
> chords which I listened to one after another. I already harbored a distrust
> of those who in family circles are called "musical" persons and still do so today
> —in the widest meaning. I have never, neither earlier or later, wanted to see
> any "principal" difference between harmony and dissonance and have never
> found it easy to accept the disciplined. Yes, in Bach and the Italians.[26]

Among other things, this long quotation is an even stronger argument
for accepting the power of those obsessive images that I have pointed
out in "A Photograph" and "The Sunset," such as the face, the partial
light, the voice, and the introverted dreamer. Quite obviously, these
images are related to the poem "Voices." Note especially the fact
that the word "shadow" is directly applied to the father here and that
death is the "shadow" at the desk in "Voices." The dizzying height,
the musical structure, equally fit into the poem and his life, as well
as the fear of being "left over" which we saw in the preceding quotation.
He repeats the link between "red sunsets and bells," and the com-
binations of fear and excitement in the roof climbing and of the despair
and beauty in the sunset may be related to major areas of ambivalence
in his life and in his writing.

The reason for these twilight ascents is his "fantastic thirst for
beauty." This thirst finds both pain and solace in the sunset that
satisfies him visually, aesthetically, yet makes his inability to express
himself more painful. The next step, the way out of his painful dilemma, is discussed in the final paragraph. "The sunset climbing was
united with musical extravangancies." It may seem repetitive to keep
reminding the reader of the complexity of Ekelöf's symbols, but it is
crucial to remember that the sunsets are "united" with both the "musical extravagancies" that he plays on the piano and with the dilemma
of his father.

The music constitutes, therefore, in one sense the romantic responses
of a young boy to beauty, and in another sense the means of escaping
his unhappy life, but a means intimately connected to the pain of his
life. This transformation of a negative father to an escapist sunset
and, finally, to a liberating music represents a cycle of alienation,

[26] *Ibid.*, pp. 167-168.

identification, and transformation which in symbolic form recurs in Ekelöf's writing. The poem "Voices" has traces of all three phases.

Returning to "An Outsider's Way," this description anticipates the narrator's artistic life. Significantly enough, the description of music has much in common with Ekelöf's father. "Disconnected," "dissonant," "endless series," these are words that belong to a description of Ekelöf's father, and, conversely, the disciplined music that is rejected is what could not be described in such terms. The combination of the identification and the transformation is related to mysticism and its anti-rational qualities, appealing, I suggest, specifically to the similarity between meaninglessness and mysticism: the impossibility of gaining understanding by verbal means.

> Above all else it was mysticism which attracted me during these years of gradual awakening, and youthful mystics are probably more troublesome and odder than somewhat older mystics. I came to detest Europe and Christianity and taught myself my "Om mani padme hum" as a protest. It was not, however, before I dared to go through the brimfire of the information desk and the card catalog at the Royal Library, an irritating enough task for a rebellious young man, because the rebellious are usually the most timid, that I got nutrition for my orientalism. There I stuffed my head full of the most obsolete facts about ruined cities, oriental art, music and literature. A book which since then has always followed me is Fox-Strangways' "Music of Hindustan," and some time I should truly like to learn how to handle a drum, next to the human voice oriental music's finest instrument.[27]

Music and mysticism are tied together in this passage and the rejection of Europe is to be expected in terms of that part of himself which is alienated. One wonders if the love of the voice, and here presumably oriental singing, has some distant connection with the father's voice. In the first chapter we saw how Ekelöf combines mysticism and music in his theory of poetry. This union grew from his childhood. The next step is to determine how the creative transition from music to poetry came about. Ekelöf went to Paris to become a musician.

> I rented, naturally in the stupidest fashion, a couple of rooms with such paper walls that I could not think of having an instrument. So there I sat in my silence and the neighbors' noise.[28]

[27] *Ibid.*, p. 168.
[28] *Ibid.*, p. 173.

He continues and explains how he began writing poetry.

Animated by the general aesthetic new and reworking that was going on around me, I decided to begin from the beginning with words. It occurred to me that I did not know anything. I took the words one by one and tried to decide their values; I put word beside word and succeeded after many trials in reaching a complete sentence—naturally not with meaning "in" but rather composed of word values. It was the hidden meaning that I sought—a kind of Alchimie du Verbe. One word has its meaning and another its own, but when they come together something curious happens with them: they get an in-between meaning: at the same time they still have their primary meanings. In a discussion on art several years ago, Grünewald expressed it this way: A water glass stands in front of me. Now I lay an orange beside it. And the water glass becomes a completely different glass. . . . This is the counterpoint of words. Seen from one direction a word's range means one thing which lies in the open daylight, seen from another direction it means something which lies—in night, in uncertainty. And poetry is just this tension-relationship—*between* the words, *between* the lines, *between* the meanings. I have, actually, learned to write like a child learns to read: B-A becomes—surprisingly enough—BA.

One must naturally also have something to say, but it is good if one begins with learning to say it and begins from the beginning. Many authors have neglected the ABC book they have within themselves, printed in 1 copy.[29]

Ekelöf began to write seriously when he could not complete the artistic development in music that he had planned. He had already written a couple of poems before this, so it might be suspected that unconsciously he was heading for this art in any case, but initially there does seem to be a direct link between music and writing.

The important point is the fact that he returns to the source of his need to write, to the point I have indicated and where he admitted a block had arisen, to the beginning, the "dognose" meaning of words. He may have performed a kind of self-analysis in this process of going back to the beginning. Indeed, considering that Ekelöf termed his first book a "suicide book" and that it was published in 1932, the reader feels certain that he must have gone through such an experience.[30] This quotation reveals that in order for him to use words as an artistic means of expression, he had to find a way of utilizing the hidden meaning that as a child he suspected in his father's use of words.

[29] *Ibid.*, p. 173-174.
[30] *Ibid.*, p. 174.

This is verified by the actual use of the image of the ABC book that previously was the symbol or the example of his inability to understand the relation between word and reality. At the very least, the parallel between "A Photograph" and "An Outsider's Way" in terms of the ABC book implies that the mature Ekelöf may have been aware of the cycle he underwent from a young child to a young artist.

I note in passing that the hidden meanings he sought, the meanings between words, corresponds to phenomenologically oriented discussion, such as my interpretation of "Voices." Bachelard, much influenced by Husserl's phenomenology, provides a key that opens into the middle space of the tension-relationship that contains for Ekelöf the essence of poetry. The reader has an opportunity to become aware of his own participation in the poem, to discover a hint of its human core, and thus discover its in-between and hidden meanings.

In general this may explain why Ekelöf's poetry often seems so difficult, sometimes incomprehensible. If, through this interaction between reader, poet, and poem, meaning becomes hidden or too abstract, the reader may think of one of Ekelöf's own images as an example of clarification. The image of the bird in the stone obviously has a wide range of meaning in Ekelöf's poetry, but it may be transposed to suit our purposes here. The word is like the stone. Its primary meaning is not dead, but it is solidified to the point that it lives in an almost stonelike limitation. The hidden meaning of the word is the bird, the life within the rock, and if we are willing and capable we can hear it and perhaps ultimately, as does Ekelöf, invoke its flight.

From the study of the three pieces of prose in this chapter, the unique "personal symbolism" of the themes and images from "Voices" as they relate to Ekelöf's life and writing begins to be understood. "A Photograph" reveals Ekelöf's sense of alienation, caused by his father's mental illness, and shows the importance to Ekelöf as a boy of his father's face, voice, and house. The boy's ability to understand the connection between words and reality is related to his father's mumbling voice. Confronted with this death-in-life paradox, the boy is driven inward and develops a love-fear attitude toward his father and a sense of estrangement from the world.

The boy identifies with his father to a limited extent, possibly because of the occasional clear moments of the father and the lack of a strong mother figure.* This identification process gradually unfolds in "The Sunset" and establishes the close association of sunsets and tolling bells with the father. The wandering main figure must return home and resolve the conflicts of his father and the "voices" before he can hear a new music and be prepared to embark for the future.

"An Outsider's Way" shows how the alienation and the identification eventually lead to the creative process. At first they take the form of music, but as Ekelöf becomes freer he goes back to his childhood and proceeds from there as an artist along the very lines established when he first learned to read within the sound of the mumbling voice of his father. Finally, the poet's theory of poetry combines music, mysticism, and the hidden meanings of words as the poetic resolution of his early years.

---

* The museum's womb-separation scene as well as the woman in the brass bed "who always used to sleep while I watched" support my argument for a weak mother figure.

III. IN AUTUMN

"and the night rests, a mirror, black
against the windowpanes."

HAVING DISCUSSED the images and themes of "Voices" and having
pointed out at least part of their historical and psychological founda-
tions, I can now turn to a few key poems in which these images and
themes appear in Ekelöf's first twenty years of poetry.

Erik Hjalmar Linder in his study of Ekelöf's writing says that Ekelöf
is particularly concerned with "the problem of reality." There is a
tension between internal and external which may be related to his
vision of reality.

> It is not on the whole easy to set a name upon Gunnar Ekelöf's closed, intro-
> verted, and deeply personal authorship, where dream and secretive music
> work together with fine intellectual analysis. He has rightly called himself
> "outsider"; another useful designation would be Romantic. It is with the
> problem of reality that he ceaselessly wrestles. Toward wholeness he strains,
> with a lively perception of the necessity of division.[1]

The tendency toward division and unity, which Linder points out,
directly relates to "Voices." Desiring unity, yet experiencing isolation and fragmentation, the voices and narrators speak from within
Ekelöf's poetry in general. It is helpful to look at his overall view of
reality in terms of two extremes and a separated midpoint. In his
early writing the extremes are most clearly seen in the romantic juxtaposition of reality and ideal. This tension is sometimes stated as life
versus dream and sometimes as life versus death. Consistently enough,
however, the poet selects a point in the middle of and separate from
such extreme attitudes, a position that may be related originally to
his ability to accept his father and his childhood but extends with
the poet's own life into the concept of the outsider, the witness, the
artist.

---

[1] Erik Hjalmar Linder, *Ny Illustrerad Svensk Litteraturhistoria* (Stockholm,
1958), 5, 725.

The poet's concerns, in the first twenty years of his writing, go from the outside world to the inside, from a longing for transformation through sunsets and music to an introverted consciousness creating and accepting its own world. This obviously does not exclude such things as sunsets and music from his later work, for he consciously retains much of his past, but it may change his attitude toward them.

The approval of physical reality, which the mature poet occasionally reaches, is centered upon the development of a sphere in which the alien, the outsider, is natural or comfortable. The transition occurs within the poet's own consciousness. There is no clear dividing line in the movement back and forth between external and internal and Ekelöf did not intend such a line to be drawn. He has stated his poetic theory in the following words: "and my whole artistic conception is to return to the source, to begin again and begin again."[2] His spiral development has preserved obsessive images by continually giving them new meanings and variations.

Beginning chronologically, *Splinters of a Volume of Poetry 1927-28* (first published in 1952) gives an early example of the problems that he faces as a young poet.

> A bell rings in the distance, monotonous and calm, suddenly a train whistle sticks its fine pin through the silence.
>
> Over the gray roofs the cloudy sky arches and the evening air drifts in through the window. The trees whisper softly among their crowns and several golden leaves fall slowly to the ground. On the smoky horizon the sun's dismal rays break through the clouds one last time.
>
> It darkens more and more.
>
> I think of everything far away. The bell that rings in the distance, monotonous and calm, calls me to a church service, I do not know when nor where. It seems to me as if I lost something I cannot be without, but I do not know what it is. A silent, impotent pain seethes up within me and permeates me, but I do not know why. I close the window. I hold my hands over my ears, but inexorably the clock's mild bells peal out from within me.[3]

The substance of this lyrical prose poem is primarily the narrator's reaction to a specific landscape. Structure and language reinforce the

---

[2] Gunnar Ekelöf, *Sent på Jorden med Appendix 1962, och En Natt Vid Horisonten* (Stockholm, 1962), p. 173.

[3] Ekelöf, *Dikter* (Stockholm, 1965), p. 10.

prosaic simplicity of the scene. The narrator first presents the country-side emphasizing its monotony by commenting on the insignificant event of a passing train. Only the words "dismal" and "monotonous" indicate a human presence. This uninvolved perspective is repeated by distant objects, the bell, the whistle, the cloudy sky. Nothing close to the narrator is really described: the whispering trees and falling leaves are suggestive but hardly represent detailed portrayal. The contrast between "everything far away," and the conclusion of the poem, "mild bells peal out from within me" is the theme: the bell is closed out but the pain with which it is associated remains.

The pealing bells are related to the passage of time as well as to the church with its concomitant metaphysical questions. The narrator's unidentified loss can and probably should be related to the church service, to God, to the narrator's longing for "something I cannot be without." In light of the later development of the poet, even the organization of the poem is relevant. The poet begins with an external scene, tries to project or imagine himself beyond it, and then is forced into a painful internal experience. The bells seem to make him aware of three worlds: the one that is not and that he lacks, the physical one in front of him, and the one that he feels inside of himself.

There are similar examples in this early collection. Number six shows him dispersing the self, and awareness of time, by momentarily replacing them with the world outside of him.

> I am no longer me; the god's meaninglessness is in me. Time stands still, the room exists no more. My thoughts' thought sways away through colorless spaces, mirroring everything.[4]

In contrast to the pain that the bell and the train caused him, the absence of physical phenomena in this poem, or the feeling of their absence, produces what I interpret to be a positive reaction. This tends to follow the pattern that distant things are good and transcendence of them is even better.

Late on the Earth was the first volume published by Ekelöf, and its title presumably possesses the negative connotations of Spengler's theory of history. The volume would be expected to be a pessimistic

---

[4] *Ibid.*, p. 9.

view of a dying world. Whether or not it is, however, it is one of the most important literary events of twentieth-century Swedish literature.

Rabbe Enckell, one of Sweden's major poets contemporary with Ekelöf, said that it was absolutely unique and had "no notable predecessors in Swedish poetry."[5] Reidar Ekner says: *"Late on the Earth* stands out all the more clearly as perhaps the most important volume of Swedish poetry that has appeared in this century . . ."[6]

While it is not my intention to put Ekelöf into any literary historical perspective, one of the reasons for the volume's significance was its use of new poetic techniques, some of which were related to surrealism. Ekelöf has commented upon this supposed connection.

> When *Late on the Earth* was winnowed out I heard: "But you are a surrealist." Glad on the whole to be anything I wrote a couple of the final poems in a kind of surrealistic style and dated them carefully enough to give the illusion that it was "automatic writing." Such small falsifications one can do to be helpful to others and naturally, most important, to oneself. But surrealism at that time had not played any great importance for me with the exception of Robert Desnos' *"Corps et Biens,"* although that book really does not belong to the movement's theological canon.[7]

Breton's statement in the 1924 *Manifestes du surréalisme* may have changed all contemporary European and Scandinavian poets to some extent. In any case the freedom that Breton suggested in the following statement may have aided Ekelöf, who was in Paris not long after this was published, in attaining a greater degree of freedom. This freedom, however, did not change his themes nor his images.

> Surréalisme, n. m. Automatisme psychique pur par lequel on se propose d'exprimer, soit verbalement, soit par écrit, soit de toute autre manière, le fonctionnement réel de la pensée. Dictée de la pensée, en l'absence de tout contrôle exercé par la raison, en dehors de toute préoccupation esthétique ou morale.[8]

Free thought processes in seemingly uncontrolled images are characteristically identified with surrealism. For this reason a poem such as Gunnar Ekelöf's "album page" whether faked automatic writing

5 Rabbe Enckell, "Det Omvända Perspektivet," *Prisma* (1950), p. 20.
6 Reidar Ekner, *I den havandes liv* (Stockholm, 1967), p. 57.
7 Ekelöf, *Sent på Jorden med Appendix 1962*, p. 170.
8 André Breton, *Manifestes du surréalisme* (nrf Paris, 1966), p. 37.

or not could be related to the "real functioning of thought" as described by Breton.

one night a long time ago and without stars, warm hands
   caressed your beautiful stars and your voice that walked over mountains
or perhaps a voice that someone walked away from and did not get its throat
   back, the inexpressible desire for a conclusion to which the fires burned
   on the mountain tops and glittered in the diamonds of wild animals in the
   high grass
one night whose waves stepped and sank over and under the sea's surface
a voice which called my name among the mountains, a tone which stepped and
   sank deserted over and under a great lonely ringing bell,
and the wind which slowly destroyed the memory of a torch put out in the
   waves on the beach of an absence where the sea never ended,
and my despair which with turned away face said goodby to someone whose
   name I forgot or the forgetfulness which sank over the sea's beach whose
   dead shellfish stared like broken eyes into the future.[9]

In spite of the dreamlike quality of the poem or because of it, the content of "album page" is consistent with Ekelöf's own life and writing. The "night" is a "long time ago" and the stars are not visible. The voice walks away, or perhaps is left behind as an echo, as a human sound without a human mind expressing it. There is a longing for a conclusion and apparently everything in the distance reflects this longing; it even burns in the eyes, the "diamonds," of the wild animals. The voice and the mountains are reported in direct relation to the narrator and the call sinks "deserted" over and under a lonely ringing bell. As the wind slowly destroys the memory of a torch going out in the waves, quite possibly the sunset, the image of the sea is repeated in connection with its endlessness.

The poem progresses from mountains to sea, and from an "inexpressible desire" to a sense of "despair." The key link to the progression is the voice positively presented in the opening and rather negatively portrayed in the conclusion. If the poem is translated into prose, its relation to Ekelöf's personal imagery can be seen.

The night, with its pleasurable associations, almost takes the narrator's voice away. Freely associating in his mind, he longs for a goal and transfers the longing to an image of fire on the mountains, or it

---

[9] Ekelöf, *Dikter* (1965), p. 22.

may be the sinking sun. Night rolls over him and the "voice," deserted, sinks beneath the ringing bell. From this point on the poem becomes negative. The wind destroys the memory of what is probably the sunset, "a torch" going "out in the waves." The image of despair is his "turned away face" that apparently cannot look at something, at someone "whose name I forgot," or at forgetfulness itself, perhaps death.

Such an interpretation, with its numerous obvious associations with the father, may involve a certain degree of conjecture on my part, but it does follow the pattern of a visible scene of night, probably a sunset, a longing and a voice without a mind which leads the narrator via a bell to a "turned away face" leading to forgetfulness and death. There may be some underlying theme in the poem of time's capacity to "forget" both the poet and the father, but I do not want to push the interpretation any farther.

Another example of the dream technique in this important volume of poetry is the poem "unrhymed sonnet" which Printz-Påhlson points out is one of the earliest examples of the "bird-in-stone image."[10] The poem, in irregular iambs, but unrhymed and with irregular syllabic count, has what Bachelard would call "labyrinthian" imagery.

> when the dream goes out it is time to waken
> my soul is finished, my star inflamed
> my red will threadbare enough to lack
> the entrusted light I dissipated
> I bury ashes under the clouds' burden
> in my thoughts' endless alleys: alone
> where my birds plunged down into earth's darkness
> and my soul steeled to its own marble image
> alone in my thoughts' endless alleys
> where the echo lags behind distant worlds
> in whose tracks I bury myself
> my one hand like death embalmed
> still waves white from the grave's black earth
> farewell to the birds which the wind has freed.[11]

The poem begins with an apparent juxtaposition between being asleep and being awake similar to the one in the poem "Written Down

[10] Göran Printz-Påhlson, *Solen i spegeln* (Stockholm, 1958), p. 105.
[11] Ekelöf, *Dikter* (1965), p. 26.

in 1932." The poem, which at first seems extremely symbolic in a rather weak fashion, coheres more effectively when the missing positive qualities to his dreams are attributed. In concrete terms, his soul may live; his star may not be inflamed, and his "red will" may be less "thread-bare" in his dreams. If he could regain his dream, he might get back his "entrusted light."

The second stanza presents a dark suffocating world which is given even greater emphasis by the repetition of the word "bury" in the third stanza. His "thoughts' thought" is a conscious state and one that is presumably negative with its "endless alleys." The plunge of the birds can be contrasted with their flight when he was dreaming. Such a suggestion is strengthened by the final stanza. His one hand waves as if that one hand were still in the land of dreams, the land of the sky rather than the reality of life with its consciousness of the grave.

The poem presents the poet's hostility to conscious life. It can be seen how the longing in that hand will one day speak as a voice from under the ground. The image presents and anticipates the use of an internal thought process within a negatively inhabited space. The contrast of a smothered or buried figure to the "distant worlds" is another of Ekelöf's personal images.

The same structural opposition of earth to sky appears in the poem "against the triangle." The prose poem begins with an image of the narrator who may have some distant connection with the pacing and muttering father.

> I have sunk from the function of human to the function of floor measurer, long enough have my tired thoughts wandered round in their own worn footprints before the bars to endless freedom.[12]

"Against the triangle" continues with frustrated wishes, night's wings, and the narrator's process of turning his eyes inward to resemble his own death mask. A hope for transformation concludes the poem.

> One day, when perhaps the solitary clock, my heart, which regularly perforates the silence and the timelessness, strikes its thirteenth beat of salvation, the organpoint will begin the long glide upward and slowly change to a thin voice which higher and higher disappears in infinity's free shell . . .
> then there will be no more stars and the lamp long since have darkened.

[12] *Ibid.*, p. 24.

His preoccupation with time and its association with the beat, the ringing bell, the clock is evident. The narrator, however, hopes for an escape from his limitations. The symbol of his unhappiness, the voice, may become a symbol of salvation.

Another example of Ekelöf's vision of the tension or conflict between earth and sky, wakefulness and sleep, occurs in the little poem "sleep and emptiness even breathing."[13] Ekner has studied the importance to Ekelöf as a boy of the eclipse in 1914. This poem is one of many that may be related to the adolescent's reaction to the darkening of the sun.[14]

> the night falls slowly without wings
> the birds go out in the air
> the wings fall to the ground
> the silence opens the wind and the wings are silent
> the stones shut
> the wind silences in the night and the stones close
>> (when the dream glassclear opened your eye you saw how
>> the flowers leaned toward the stones)

Written in appropriately falling trochees and dactylls and partially rhymed, this is a more subtle poem than some of the others in *Late on the Earth*. The poem's progression is similar to Ekelöf's early evolution, from night to a dream of the earth. It begins with the night's birdless descending, that is, night settling down upon him like a great bird whose wings he cannot see or hear. The descending night forces the birds to land and they, in the dusk, seem to go out like candles; their wings fall to the ground. As the wind begins, the narrator notices the absence of the birds, notices the earth itself. The sky darkens and the stones themselves seem to shrink, to close. Everything gradually disappears in the darkness, but then the dream, from sleep or from imagining what cannot be seen, opens the narrator's eyes and he sees the closeness of the flowers and the stones, already symbols to Ekelöf. Here, the flowers seem to symbolize beauty and the stones are the earth.

Faced, even in soft and almost romantic terms, with an earth and a life that close down upon him and block his vision and his life, he

---

[13] *Ibid.*, p. 26.
[14] Ekner, "Det mörknar över vägen," *Svensk Litteratur tidskrift*, 31 (1968), 3-11.

must look beyond the earth in order to discover new meaning and new depths. This particular poem anticipates his later method of looking at the external world and transposing it into the acceptability of a dream or of a "beyond." At this point, however, the emphasis is placed first upon the external world. The life within the poet-narrator is included parenthetically, even though its insight recreates for him the external world.

To conclude this section on *Late on the Earth*, excerpts from one final poem suggest how Ekelöf combines his intense sensation of displacement with his split vision of earth and sky, waking and sleeping, or comparable divisions of man's condition, into a positive and a negative.

The "cosmic sleepwalker" is a dark vision concluding with the theme of the book, "It is late on the earth."[15] Much of the poem's imagery falls into categories that I have suggested are typical.

> the withered leaves fall slowly down over broken eyes
> which stare forever into the sky's collapse
> the withered leaves lie softly over the blind child's
> eyes and over his hands which grope in sleep
> and seek shellfish among the beach's stones
> and in the sunset's incest lives still the memory of the time
> when I myself was blind as a child and my dreams
> were a child's dreams . . .
> . . . .
>
> distant as a restless thought in the stones' gray heads which since time immemorial blindly meditate upon the invisible . . .
> . . . .
>
> alone alone as a pillar on the plain and blind as a child whose loneliness the infinite mother slowly sings to sleep tired and meaningless as an answer without question or a question without answer . . .

Bachelard's concept of inhabited space, specifically the shellfish, makes certain sections of this poem more comprehensible. The poet's unsatisfied and critical vision is indicated in terms of images recognizable as negative: "broken eyes," and "the sky's collapse." Both Bachelard and Baudouin indicate that blindness in literature is a form of introversion. In Ekelöf's case there is the parallel with his father's unseeing

---

[15] Ekelöf, *Dikter* (1965), pp. 33-34.

eyes. The child's search in his sleep for an image representing home, the shellfish, and the association of the image with the sunset hint at the degree to which these images were enmeshed in the poet's subconscious life.

"Cosmic sleepwalker" continues the conflict between dream-life and conscious-life; it presents an image of the near versus the far perspective, and uses stones as a central reference for thought. The childhood loneliness, the resultant introversion, and the turn toward an "infinite mother" instead of an earthly one, give a cluster of images probably directly related to Ekelöf's own life.

Printz-Påhlson refers to "cosmic sleepwalker" as one example of Ekelöf's use of dreams and says they are an "unbelievably common motive" in Ekelöf's poetry.[16] Printz-Påhlson feels that Ekelöf's use of the dream can be related to a category suggested by Breton in which the dream is a part of an attitude that highly values lesser states of consciousness, such as sleep and dreams. Dreams in Ekelöf's poetry, according to Printz-Påhlson, "have above all else the power to 'transform'" and are a "necessary condition of a tolerable existence." While these ideas are strongly supported by my own study, his suggestion that "the dream in Ekelöf as a material for metaphors almost never appears as a land or a landscape . . . but very often as a living being"[17] fits in less well with my conclusions.

Ekner, while discussing poetry of a later date, says of Ekelöf's poetry about nature: "It is always a synthesis of landscape and the experience of the landscape, and it is less the drawing of a landscape than it is the attitude of the soul, the condition in life, and self analysis."[18]

In general this attitude is closer to my own position, for Ekelöf often looks to dreams for landscape description. If this seems paradoxical, look again at both "cosmic sleepwalker" and "unrhymed sonnet." These poems tend to give human qualities to objects and substances. This tendency develops as dreams, trees, birds, and shellfish are given human attributes. Dreams are often the means by which this anthropomorphism occurs. "Voices" is merely one example of

---

[16] Printz-Påhlson, *Solen i spegeln*, p. 97.
[17] *Ibid.*, p. 99.
[18] Ekner, *I den havandes liv*, p. 25.

a vision of an inanimate but living universe. Printz-Påhlson's awareness of the organic nature of Ekelöf's primitivism, an organic nature that aids his concept of evolution, reinforces this position.

The dream is particularly important to Ekelöf's early poetry. In *Dedication* (1934), his next volume of poetry, we find examples of either union or conflict between dream and reality. One poem, "Between five and seven," seems to be based upon a premise of sleeplessness.[19]

> I turn in my room sleeping and waking.
>   I have a cloud in my arms but no dreams.
> I turn in my room which is dirty with darkness.
>   My lamplight grows paler and paler.
> The dawn spins slowly its thoughtless weave over the window.
>   The cold hangs shivering in the curtains.
> I turn away from the questions and answers
>   When the mailman empties the mailbox full of meaningless syllables.
> Outside the windows stare emptily at the dawn's ice.
>   The handcarts dream dreams of being held outside.
> The lamps stand quietly like holiday candles in the fog:
>   The iron's lilies give up the ghost in the iron's flame.
> The coldness of the cosmos sinks slowly over the earth.
>   The houses save their poor warmth deep under grayclad surfaces.
> The air is corpse pale and the city's stones are dead forever:
>   The city's stones sleep peacefully with timeless dreams in their hearts.
> It is stones which rest heavily under men's sparse steps,
>   Stones which have only weight to hope for.
> It is stones which can only be themselves,
>   Stones which have to understand nothing.

The poem suggests a man exhausted from "sleeping and waking" whose lamp has been on all night while he struggled with insomnia. Dawn finally arrives. "Between five and seven" seems to be the period during which he sleeps and wakes, possibly watches the dawn, writes, then goes back to bed. Because he cannot sleep solidly he has a "cloud . . . but no dreams" in his arms. The room is partially dark; the lamplight begins to disappear in the dawn's light. Instead of looking at the room, or perhaps after he has gone to sleep and awakened again, the narrator looks out the window. The handcarts and lamps catch his attention. It is difficult to be certain about the meaning of "The

---

19 Ekelöf, *Dikter* (1965), p. 40.

iron's lilies" but possibly it refers to the iron lanterns or streetlights which fade in the light of the sun as it burns, although without warmth. The coldness of the earth becomes visible in the dawnlight. As the narrator sees the houses, the air, the stones of the buildings, and the streets, he envies the stones. His restless night and the vision of the cold and indifferent world outside make him want to be a stone. Although stone is generally negative in Ekelöf's poetry, here it is positive.

In the implied natural state of stones, there is a suggestion that at a certain level even stones are in a harmonious state. This is opposed to the narrator himself who is alienated from everything that he sees, and presumably from himself if insomnia is any indication. Both a satisfactory life and the happiness of dreams evade him. The intensity of his frustration and bitterness could hardly be more effectively expressed than to suggest that stones fit more comfortably into this world than he does. This type of reduction implies that the narrator sees death itself as a preferable condition to his own life.

In several "Elegies" Ekelöf continues to employ dreams, and to ponder their relation to reality. During this part of his life Ekelöf seeks figures with whom he can identify. One man who meets his needs is Carl Johan Stagnelius, a Swedish Romantic poet who in the short twenty-nine years of his life (1793-1823) managed to write poetry ranging from the transcendental to the sensual. Coming from a religious family, Stagnelius lived in isolation and apparently was an alcoholic clerk during his last years in Stockholm. In a tradition rich with alienated writers, Stagnelius is one of the most prominent examples. Stagnelius's Romanticism and the range of his poetry make him an excellent figure of identification for the young Ekelöf. Ekelöf wrote two elegies to Stagnelius in *Dedication* which touch on dreams.[20]

> Say bitter waves, do you cry for men or gods?
> Say waves, you who wash away the dreamt tracks of both.
> Say waves, you who hide all that is written
> in life's water and in time's sand.

Failure of man to escape, of any hope to escape human limitations, is often considered in terms of man's dreams. Positively, the dream

[20] *Ibid.*, p. 46.

may occur in reference to the sea or the sky in Ekelöf's poetry. There are usually negative connotations in the dreams of stones or other basically earthbound objects. In the second elegy to Stagnelius, Ekelöf gives an example of the earth's relation to dreams.

> And the earth sinks down wasted and dreamless,
> Blesses the emptiness and prays to the darkness . . .
> And autumn's dark wings sink into the world, heavy
> With dreams and with life which never wakened . . .

This gives one the feeling that autumn is dragged down because of the weight of dreams that were never realized. Whether the emphasis is upon dream and man's inability to attain his dreams, or upon time and man's incapacity to deal with physical existence, in these early years Ekelöf sees human existence in dualistic terms with occasional moments of resolution or union. One of the most powerful poems in *Dedication* illustrates the temporary balance of this dualistic conflict. Although still Romantically oriented, the poem anticipates the poet's actual future direction.

> Song to Ease Pain[21]
> Go to the beach, mumbling in the wind,
> Go to the beach's stones with your anguish.
> You see, there is the sea, here is the land:
> Reality! You can touch it with your hand.
> Lift a stone from the world's heavy heart,
> Weigh it in your hand and let it fall.
> Lift a stone and throw it in the water,
> Let a lifeless memory sink down in forgetfulness.
> You see now that the beach was a rosary, fallow prayers,
> Pray for greenery, life and gladness, stone for stone:
> In your mouth shall songs grow, stronger than the wind,
> And your soul shall bear feelings, deeper than happiness.
> You shall still the storms in the world's heart,
> You shall braid the lightning to simple wreathes,
> And when the weight and death of all stones is expiated
> You shall walk free to your rich tranquillity.

The commitment of this poem is almost militant with its imperatives and its generally falling trochees and dactylls. It is a poem centered on substances—the wind, the stones of the beach, the land and the

---

[21] *Ibid.*, p. 63.

sea—yet dealing again with a narrator's "anguish." His anguish is resolved after he points out the dualism, "there is the sea, here is the land." The narrator finds himself on the beach with the reality of earth, yet looking out to the sea, a symbol of freedom and mystery, perhaps even infinity.

The world of reality seems to be represented by the stones that may weigh down both the earth and the narrator with their "lifeless memory." If the throwing of these stones represents casting prayers, as the beach itself, "fallow prayers," may somehow be an altar before the sea, the sea offers "forgetfulness." "Life and gladness, stone for stone," however, are the things prayed for, and the narrator becomes priestlike. The final lines envision this priest-singer as a being who "still[s] the storms," and who "braids[s] the lightning." His task will be done when, with his songs, he has expiated "the weight and death of all stones," and the implication may be that his "rich tranquillity" will mean walking into the sea, although that is by no means certain.

The significant point of the poem is that it commits the narrator to his "songs." It implies the painful impossibility of true expiation, yet suggests that poetry is his chosen means of dealing with "reality." The poem may also indicate the poet's own awareness of his real means of transformation. Previously, there have been images of the sky, of voices and birds disappearing in it. These images were the ones in which the poet experienced his sense of transformation, of escape from the despair and pain of reality and mortality. The source for changing himself is now more directly related to his own capacity. The imagery is more "earthly," yet the narrator is positive. This movement away from the extreme tension between dream and reality and toward an acceptance of life, or at least a poetic means of easing the tension, is continued in the next volume, *The Sorrow and the Star* (1936).

As the title indicates, the poet's experience is still polarized, but the poem "The Tree"[22] shows the narrator attempting to deal with physical limitation.

> Sick is my heart's tree
> its arms imprisoned by the storm,
> bony, longing, passionate,

[22] *Ibid.*, p. 67.

seeking freedom's windless space.
Oh what help is spring
and greenery's fleeting promise
when the calm, the happiness is lacking
and the winds give me everything painful?
When like a mocking laugh
echoing against the slashed islets
every word, every lie in the world
reaches me carried by the winds . . .

Just as the solitary one, living
shackled among the dreaming, sleeping
stands, in his own crookedness imprisoned,
whipped into scorn of the murmuring storm,
there, the furthest pine on the rocky islet
stuck to the cliff,
cannot grow to freedom,
may not breathe,
does not want to fall,
cannot flee.

The poem immediately establishes the metaphor of the narrator's heart as a tree lacking happiness and tortured by the lies of the world. The second stanza defines the paralyzed state of the tree, its unwillingness to die, and its inability to flee. The image is essentially a natural one, and, apart from his initial identification with the tree, the poet lets it dominate the poem. Somewhat atypically, the structure of the poem is built upon a progression from inward to outward.

The earthbound tree suggests that the poet may be identifying more precisely the qualities that alienate him and, upon occasion, he is willing to describe these qualities in a more realistic and less Romantic way. The tree's dilemma is a real and physical one in contrast with a poem such as "unrhymed sonnet" with its bird in the sky and the single hand reaching from the ground.

Printz-Påhlson refers to a long prose poem in *The Sorrow and the Star* "which is called The Dream and it shows clearly the 'romantic' longing for some indeterminate distance which marks the volume as a whole."[23] There is no doubt that the dream continues to represent this "longing," and that it is a major portion of the book with the dream

---

[23] Printz-Påhlson, *Solen i spegeln*, p. 101.

"placed in clear opposition to reality."[24] But, as Printz-Påhlson points out, the dream-motif decreases in usage after this volume. The particular context of the transition is suggested by "The Tree" and by another poem, "Dawn."[25]

When the night has counted
its hours
with the pulse's anguished beat,
when sleepless dawn has paled
and darkness's last
grinning mockery has scattered,
then I stand in the window,
waiting long
the saving day . . .

When the morning lifts
its wings
from the fog's streaming sea,
then I see in the window
only the land gray and still
and the trees hard, closed
around the road, mockingly empty . . .

Dawn, how indifferently
you allow the swarming terrors
to change to loneliness!

Day, how pale and mutely
you allow your ashes
to be thrown over things!
It is as if the stones,
the fields and hills
turned their backs to me!

The remaining swallows
grow quiet in the trees:
Nothing more drives
the listless soul to flight.

This poem gives the reader the opportunity to compare similar subject matters from different periods. The earlier poem "Between five and seven" deals with the same theme of insomnia and the narrator's vision of the world at dawn. We recall that "Between five and

[24] *Ibid.*, p. 101.
[25] Ekelöf, *Dikter* (1965), p. 74.

seven" portrayed the narrator as deprived of dreams and almost envious of the stones that he sees, because they "sleep peacefully with timeless dreams in their hearts."

Significantly, the dream is not even mentioned in "Dawn." This is a remarkable deletion in light of Ekelöf's thematic development up to this point and given the subject of sleep. The poem is concerned with the dispersal of night; the day represents salvation. The concluding stanzas of the poem emphasize the indifference of the day, but an indifference that is unquestionably preferable to sleeplessness and night.

The transition in imagery helps in seeing the depth of the development suggested. Night is described in terms of pulse and grinning mockery; both are elements possibly related to the negative childhood images of the bells and the face. Conversely, day is given wings; the fog becomes a sea; both are often positive images. The poem has much in common with "Written Down in 1932." Loneliness is the result of the daylight, as it is in "Written Down," but here the loneliness is preferable to night. Just exactly why this is so is not understood until the final line of the poem. Before that final line, however, the narrator sees the stones. The stones were enviable in "Between five and seven." Here, "the stones, the fields and hills" turn their backs to the narrator.

The final stanza becomes more complex when related to a wider range of Ekelöf's poetry. Birds are usually positive images and often symbolize freedom and the means of escaping from this life to a dreamed of "distant land." The swallows in "Dawn" have settled in the trees. This should be a negative action for the narrator, but he feels that the quiet of the birds allows his "listless soul" to rest.

It seems probable that the "swarming terrors" of night have been driving the narrator's soul to flight, and at the same time the flight of the swallows, presumably flying at dawn, have also been doing this. Thus, "nothing more" implies that the swallows, representatives of the frustrations of ideals, were the last thing bothering him. Momentarily freed of fear and of longing for the ideal, his soul is now quiet. This simple desire for a moment's tranquillity seems more realistic than the envy of stones that were found in "Between five and seven."

The role of reality and dream in Ekelöf's poetry continues to be defined in the prose poem "The Dream" in which the narrator says,

"Only the one who still can dream can live. I who believed in reality—
a part of me is dead within me because none exists."[26] These lines,
as does the poem "Dawn," indicate that part of the poet still wants
to be a dreamer, but that part of him is also learning how to deal with
the disappointment of reality. Printz-Påhlson's thesis is that Ekelöf
develops an evolutionary primitivism, a preference for the unaware
state of primitive man, perhaps for a state of unconsciousness. Related to this belief is apparently the hope that man will gradually
evolve. Ekelöf's early evolution leads him to a contained pessimism,
a recognition that if life or growth is possible it must come from a root
of despair and futility.

The long poem "The Summer Night"[27] demonstrates this position
and seems to be the clearest and one of the most poignant statements
by Ekelöf of the pain of dreams and the frustration of existence. It
focuses completely on nature and demonstrates within it the life of
dreams and the death of life. In its final lines it anticipates the best
of the middle years of Ekelöf's poetry.

> A scent of autumn and fallen leaves on dusky paths
>   becomes silent music
> for every cloudy wind which slowly effaces
>   a human dream.

The transition to reality is definitely stated in Ekelöf's next book
Buy the Blind Man's Song (1938). Ekner says of it:

> When the poet uses a blind beggar as his narrator, he has with that action
> left the private and placed himself in the middle of the swarming street with
> the noise of streetcars and automobiles, phenomena which were unthinkable
> in *The Sorrow and the Star*.[28]

While the volume is heavily weighted with contemporary references
to the fearful development of Germany, the style of the poetry is one
of an increasingly condensed imagery, a lighter and sometimes comic
tone. The title poem illustrates the character of the book. Written
in irregular iambs and anapests, its smoothness and rapidity suit a
two and three stress line quite comfortably. It is rhymed, but sometimes

---

[26] *Ibid.*, p. 83.

[27] *Ibid.*, p. 91.

[28] Ekner, *I den havandes liv*, p. 32.

on alternate lines, sometimes in couplets. The language is concrete with an emphasis on nouns and verbs that directly relate to each other.

> Buy the blind man's song[29]
> I've stood here all day long
> and had my blue
> eyeglasses on
> and the sign about stonechip and powderspeck
> hung on brass links around my neck
> and the white hat in my hand
> and the warning band on my arm!
>
> The seeing, who are swindled
> and swindle and cheat and trust,
> may decorate their arms
> with white, black, and brown armbands . . .
>
> Buy the blind man's song!

By including a reference to Hitler's regime and by its modern pessimistic attitude, the poem obviously rejects idealism, yet it retains Ekelöf's essential imagery and his search for resolution if not transformation.

> Yet: this to live
> what is it more than to fumble
> forward in a sparse
> and secret light,
> to grope cautiously
> toward the day in the east,
> to interpret these voices
> to what they mean,
> to be what one is.

"Being what one is" differs from Ekelöf's earlier romantic longing by its commitment to immediate reality. The poem concludes by mocking those who believe in or live in the land of "Once upon a time." By fumbling "forward in a sparse and secret light," the poem reveals Ekelöf's new method of living and almost willingly limits the framework of existence to the physical present. The third of "Three Elegies"[30] repeats this commitment.

[29] Ekelöf, *Dikter* (1965), p. 99.
[30] *Ibid.*, p. 109.

And still it is here I want to live,
here I want to settle,
here on the earth, with men.
What wonder if I linger long
and tightly cling.

Buy the Blind Man's Song is often considered a transitional volume, the beginning of a paradoxical commitment to life. Reidar Ekner says of its final poem:

"In the final poem, Coda I, earlier called Confidence, there is formulated for the first time a conviction which is going to be central to the poetry of the next few years, the belief that darkness in time will diminish, that life's red Ariadne's thread will appear in the weave, that life needs those "who want a meaning."[31]

Everything has its time, thus even this darkness
and these catacombs—finally
life needs those who want a meaning.

What would be the weave of events without
the red thread, Ariadne's thread,
invisible now and then, but always woven in.

And even now, in these times of death,
something remains: that he alone
who serves life itself will live on.

Ferry Song (1941) is considered Ekelöf's "breakthrough" volume, and its significance can hardly be underestimated, for although much of what appears in *Ferry Song* is anticipated in the earlier volumes, the clarity and power of the opening poem indicates at least part of what has happened in the intervening years. The poem, "Open it, Write" is a commitment to writing.

In the book of translations by Muriel Rukeyser and Leif Sjöberg, Ekelöf is quoted as saying of the title of the program poem—"Tag och skriv" [literally "Take and write"], "Augustine says, Tag och läs and take for good what you read." I mean with "Tag och skriv! Read, and make it your own, give it your own expression."[32] The poem is a statement of a newly discovered artistic power based upon the dilem-

---

[31] Ekner, *I den havandes liv*, p. 33.

[32] Muriel Rukeyser and Leif Sjöberg, trans., *Selected Poems of Gunnar Ekelöf* (New York, 1967), p. 104.

ma and the tensions that have been functioning throughout the study. The poet Erik Lindegren perceives the same consciousness of the self in relation to reality which I am emphasizing:

> In the next volume of poetry, *Ferry Song*, which came out in 1941, we witness how the Ekelöfian doubt of reality turns toward the consciousness of the "I" itself. *Ferry Song* is totally marked by the battle of someone who "wants a meaning"; for the most part that is the problem attacked, radical reckoning with the self, at once surer and more abstract than his previous works; one thinks inevitably of the later Eliot. But the problem is completely Ekelöf's own, and it is fascinating to follow how the interplay between a feeling for life and a need for truth drive him step after step down mysticism's narrowest road.[33]

Although Lindegren sees the same self-awareness that I find, he sees it in terms of abstraction and mysticism. How these various terms come together becomes clearer in the major poems of this volume. "Open it, Write" introduces the philosophical force behind Ekelöf's new perspective on the world and presents new symbols to give additional ranges of meaning to his own writing. A more personal statement of the result of this temporary plateau of security attained by Ekelöf is "Euphoria."

Because of the significance of *Ferry Song* and of "Open it, Write," it may be helpful to supply some of the critical information surrounding it. Sjöberg has analyzed "Open it, Write" and in his opening comments he presents some of the basic critical issues related to *Ferry Song*.

> When Ekelöf's *Ferry Song* was published in 1941, it was in some respects a return to the sphere and manner of *Late on the Earth* with its use of thoughts and elements from various sources. This allusion technique has been extended and developed further in *Ferry Song* where there are thoughts from Buddhism, Taoism, mystic writers, folklore, and modern rationalism. Partly because of this technique Ekelöf's name was linked with Eliot's. Some critics have attempted to establish Ekelöf's indebtedness to Eliot, but as Kjell Espmark has shown, it appears likely that Eliot's influence can be reduced to questions about technique and verse style. He agrees that Ekelöf's words are valid: "The fact remains that what I have to say is entirely different from what Eliot says in his poems." It is somewhat embarrassing for some Swedish critics that Ekelöf had to point this out himself. Ekelöf's art of pre-Christian and

---

[33] Erik Lindegren, "Gunnar Ekelöf: en modern mystiker," *Kritiskt 40-tal* ed. K. Vennberg and W. Aspenström (Stockholm, 1948), p. 297.

post-Christian mysticism, i.e., non-Christian, must of necessity differ widely
from Eliot's thought, at least from "Ash-Wednesday" on.
In *Ferry Song* Ekelöf presents "a third position, the objective one."[34]

Kjell Espmark has apparently resolved the debate of Eliot's influence
on Ekelöf in a fine critical article establishing that Ekelöf's translations
of Eliot were written after the relevant works and that the "allusion"
technique was apparent in Ekelöf's writing from the beginning.

Apart from the critics, Ekelöf himself has stated of *Ferry Song*,
"The circle had been closed; the long schooling was over."[35] The fruition
of his work lies in such poems as "Open it, Write" and "Euphoria."
Sjöberg's analysis of "Open it, Write" clarifies what Sjöberg calls
Ekelöf's new "third" position, an attitude I have related to his view-
point as an outsider and artist.

According to Sjöberg the first movement of the poem presents Ekelöf's rational objective—"I sing of the only thing that can redeem,
the only practical, the same for all." (See p. 140 for poem.) This
movement is a response to the exhortation of the title, a counterpart
of Saint Augustine's "tolle lege." In the second movement the speaker
takes the form of a timeless mythological bird. It is from this viewpoint
that "Only as witnesses do men exist." He sees man as a battlefield,
two antithetical drives. "We might come to think of the two forces
that Freud saw in human life, viz., the life instinct and the death instinct."[36] The third movement deals with the I, the nature of the self,
a self that basically has no free will. The fourth section deals with the
eternal conflict. The I "has such paradoxical, opposing features as
at the same time being simple and double, obscure and light."[37]

The struggle of life is eternal. Sjöberg relates this tension to the
Yin and Yang, not dualistic forces, but opposing forces which together
produce the rhythm of life.

> The secret balance of these forces is seen by the poet as the Virgin. . . . She
> is the third totally independent and unconnected point of view. That is why,

---

[34] Leif Sjöberg, "Gunnar Ekelöf's 'Tag och Skriv,'" *Scandinavian Studies*, 35
(Nov. 1963), 307.

[35] *Ibid.*, p. 314.

[36] *Ibid.*, p. 316.

[37] *Ibid.*, p. 317.

to our eyes, she seems always to be wavering. She points to an absolute ideal, independence and freedom, far beyond good and evil.[38]

The fifth movement according to Sjöberg's commentary emphasizes the necessity of perceiving the point of balance.

Ferry Song itself concludes with the two lines "I sing of the only thing that can redeem, the only practical, the same for all." (For some unexplained reason Rukeyser and Sjöberg translate the same lines differently. At the conclusion of "Euphoria," where the lines are re-printed, they print, "I sing the only thing that expiates, the only practical, for all alike.") Sjöberg says the poem "Open it, Write" is addressed to this thesis and that the answer is "obliteration." Man can perceive a higher power, however, if he is willing to renounce the self and its claims.

Sjöberg's analysis of the poem substantiates the basic trend toward a modified mysticism via a subtle affirmation of the self but using negative terms. Thematically, the poem seems to me to be a more complex version of the "Song to Ease Pain" which, as a commitment to writing, appeared in *Dedication*. The difficulty lies in determining the exact nature and relation of this newly discovered "objective" position to Ekelöf's earlier poetry and, thus, to this particular poem. The poem does present a new vision of reality while retaining Ekelöf's basic themes "Of life, of the living, Of death, of the dead."

The objective position discussed by Sjöberg was present in a structural sense in Ekelöf's earlier works. The narrator of "The Sunset" functions as a "witness." The essay "A Photograph" suggests that the young Ekelöf was a witness to a man who had in some sense become an ultimate witness, a man capable of nothing else.

The method of reaching this objective vision is the result of necessity. In order to live with his negative and alienated view of the physical world on one side and his longing for a harmonious and fulfilling "distant land" on the other, Ekelöf was forced to find a middle ground. This ground is the area of the paradox and the pure witness.

> He who wants salvation, he is already damned.
> Denial? No, the profoundest faith,
> the one that can be owned when you believe in nothing

[38] *Ibid.*, p. 318.

the one that can be owned only when you know:
I do not lie, there is no lie in me
and truth is far from me (I am far from me).

Naturally, this has much to do with oriental thought, but it is also a consistent pattern in Ekelöf's writing. As if to verify his own awareness of this imagery and the split that lies behind it, notice the way he formulates the imagery.

There is no strength other than inner strength
that from the outer comes
from that mysterious thing that moves up there
shines through those vaguely self-lit clouds
streams over you in its galvanic force.

The longing once again is located above him and seems to possess qualities similar to a sunset, "self-lit clouds." Contrasted with this image is the opposite attraction, the force that tries to draw him down, to hold him, to weaken him.

There is weakness other than inner weakness
that from the outer comes
from that mysterious thing that moves down there
shape-shifting, dark-bulging,
threatening, magnetic.

These are more than "heaven" and "hell" terms to Ekelöf. The split that they indicate in his perception of reality should be clear by now; therefore, it is the resolution, the new objective position that needs closer observance. The "Virgin" is his new symbol and theoretically establishes a new meaning of what Ekelöf now calls the "dragon" and the "knight," names that comfortably correspond to the sense of alienation and the longing for transformation previously revealed. The Virgin's final appearance in the poem serves as a focal point.

You emerge for the one who penetrates the battle.
You vanish before the one who discovers you
for he disappears in you:
A door that opens, a road that wanders away.
On the way, a single shape diminishing.
The same shape that wanders off and disappears,
again and again the same
who again and again disappears:

The "Virgin" is given an abstract identification in the poem itself, but she becomes an important symbol in Ekelöf's poetry, and as such has been discussed by various critics. Ekner relates the image to a sculpture group by Bernt Notkes and further connects the trio to the Spanish civil war in which the "knight" came to save the people from the "dragon," yet it was in fact the people who lost. Ekner says of the Virgin:

> She is, as Lindegren expresses it, a symbol for "life's innermost being, its elu-siveness and innocence." Power streams out of her stillness. She is violated, yet she is inviolable, she sacrifices her life, and still she lives. The Virgin-symbol shifts forms in Ekelöf's poetry, and every new metamorphosis her exterior undergoes is in some degree dependent upon new impressions from the poet's path.[39]

Ekner hints here at the depth of the "Virgin's" shifting form, for, while her various incarnations reflect the developing poet's life, I suggest that she herself is a new form of one of Ekelöf's primary symbols. The reader will recall from "The Sunset" the narrator who must go home to the "well known door," a phrase repeated several times in that passage, and possibly connected to "a door that opens" in this poem. Again, in "The Sunset," while the narrator is in the museum with the woman, the terrible face meets them continuously anew "always the same." The construction of the image, although it deals with a face, is not unlike the one above.

In the same essay, the description of the period after the "stranger's" death is similar to the figure of the disappearing Virgin, especially when it can be related to the essay "The Photograph" with its conclusion of the father who "still haunts."

> For years he was as someone whom one has already said goodby to, someone one recently has been separated from, and who goes his way and whose face becomes more and more indistinct, soon a disappearing memory.

These parallels, as subtle as they may be, seem to indicate a connection to the Virgin, perhaps only a hint of her, but enough so to suggest that her origins psychologically and imagistically are related to the figure of the "stranger," the father from Ekelöf's own life and consistently used in his writing. It is probable that both real and unreal

---

[39] Ekner, *I den havandes liv*, p. 52.

figures that had characteristics in common with the stranger appealed to Ekelöf, and they will be found throughout his work.

What meaning can be gained from this particular parallel? By his description of the "Virgin," the poet has united an image, previously associated with negative aspects of his childhood and gradually integrated into his writing in both positive and negative forms, with a new symbol, a symbol of transcendent mystery, and presumably a symbol for man to step back and renounce power, to survive as witness, as artist rather than either enemy or ally.

Pursuing this transition to a more abstract level is fruitful. If the evidence of the three essays and of poems such as "Song to Ease Pain" and this poem, "Open it, Write," is accepted, poetry is a means of positively reacting to the world, a method whereby the poet succeeds at least in accepting the world around him, even if he is not capable of transforming himself or the physical limitations of the world. The image of the "Virgin" not only structurally corresponds by her description to Ekelöf's established pattern of viewing reality in terms of two extremes and his search for a balanced vision between them, but that image contains seeds from a negative heritage. This new image, enriched by its past, is used to indicate a commitment to writing, an action of survival and of possible self- and world-transformation. It must be assumed that it is not accidental that the symbol chosen to represent such a commitment is not only built from the poet's own life, but that it is a traditional symbol of innocence and of the creation of life.

My explanation of this transition is relatively limited and drawn from a narrow framework of specific poems. Lindegren finds this new self-acceptance on the part of the poet elsewhere in the volume. In discussing the poem "I believe in the solitary man" (translated by Rukeyser and Sjöberg as "I believe in individual man himself"), Lindegren says,

> The mystic who walks "the wide and inner way" and who never renounces
> his freedom's silent conditions is in his own way always solid—
> > The one who does that shall never be cast out.
> > The one who does that shall forever be built in.
> > The impractical is the only practical in the long run.

Ekelöf had reached this result by accepting himself in a deeper way than before, by, in the true poet's fashion, transforming man's weakness to his strength.[40]

Lindegren's description suits accurately what I would call Ekelöf's negative affirmation. The accuracy is especially impressive in the sense that building his weakness to his strength is exactly what Ekelöf has done. *Ferry Song*, Ekelöf's breakthrough volume is rich with materials that substantiate the transition I am emphasizing. The entire first section of the volume is a proclamation of the faith in the "odd," the paradox. The connection between old imagery and new, as well as this imagery's relation to Ekelöf's new attitude can quickly be seen.

The theme of the volume is the value that death gives to life. In the poem "Oh holy death. You who give life a meaning," Ekelöf says, "Life's meaning: In the face of death to seek a meaning for life." This necessity not only involves acceptance of life but, in a limited sense, transformation of it. There is another example of an interesting parallel in the poem "Demon and Angel."[41] It begins:

> The balcony door opens.
> There he stands at the bannister, turned toward the view,
> the stranger, he with the turned away face . . .

The moment there is another "door," again opening, the reader should be curious to see who comes out of it. The "turned away face" is not new, especially in association with "the stranger." It may be relevant to note that the father's terrifyingly empty eyes once looked at him, and now, assuming the figures have some connection, they look away, in this case a positive result.

"Demon and Angel" concludes with the lines: "You see how vision and landscape efface one another: The eternal puzzle." The puzzle of landscape and vision is Ekelöf's own; what he once found clearly separated, he now finds joined, and often joined by images from his own life.

This transition can be extended to include Ekelöf's perspective on the individual human being. Lindegren summarizes his impression of Ekelöf's new attitude in this way.

[40] Lindegren, "Gunnar Ekelöf en modern mystiker," p. 301.
[41] Ekelöf, *Dikter*, p. 134.

If one wants to choose a citation which will briefly summarize Ekelöf's new vision of the individual's condition of life, one would perhaps pause before this:

> The solitary is dead, live the solitary!
> He lives who has courage to be dead,
> to be what he is: A third,
> something in between,
> still a nameless man outside.[42]

This quotation by Lindegren effectively portrays Ekelöf's attitude. This new condition is part of a newly developing group of symbols closely related to those that Ekelöf used before he was capable of verifying and identifying himself as some "nameless man outside." The unique quality of this "outsider" figure is that he accepts, he likes his position. The concept of the "third" person, the Virgin, and eventually "something else" becomes of profound importance psychologically to Ekelöf's poetry. The final poem in this volume, "Euphoria," shows in clear detail but in more realistic terminology the transition in Ekelöf's attitude toward life and poetry.

The opening poem "Open it, Write" is a commitment to art, to poetry as a means of attaining purity, of attempting to cross over the river of death, in a clearly limited sense, by poetry. The volume is in essence the process of crossing the river by accepting death, by affirming it in terms of one's own self, and by building upon that affirmation. The final poem *enacts* the opening poem. "Euphoria" shows us the acceptance of death and the artist's psychological and mystical attempt at rising beyond that limitation. The poet of "Euphoria" has crossed the river of self-acceptance.

Again in this poem there is imagery that closely parallels the imagery of the essays and indicates Ekelöf's perspective upon his own and man's condition. The poem's narrator is a second person "you" almost as if to emphasize the poet's partially objective vision of himself. He primarily addresses himself, then, perhaps, his readers as "you." Differing from most of the poetry in the volume, "Euphoria" is realistic and personal. Written in free verse, it may be symbolic, yet its language is not abstract.

---

[42] Lindegren, "Gunnar Ekelöf, en modern mystiker," p. 301.

You sit in the garden alone with a notebook, a sandwich, a flask and a pipe.
It is night but so calm that the light burns without a tremor,
spreads its reflection over the rough-hewn table
and glitters in bottle and glass.

You take a swig, a bite, you fill your pipe and light it.
You write a line or two and stop to meditate
the streak of sunset red that strides toward the morning red,
the sea of wild-chervil, foaming green-white in summer-night dusk,
not a moth near the light but choruses of gnats in the oak,
leaves standing still on the sky . . . And the aspen that rustles in stillness:
The whole of nature strong in love and death around you.

As if this were the last evening before a long, long journey;
The ticket in one's pocket and at last everything packed.
And one can sit and feel the distant country's nearness,
feel how all things are in all things, at once end and beginning,
feel that here and now are both leaving and arrival,
feel death and life strong, like wine within one!

Yes: to be one with night, one with myself, with the light's flare
that looks me in the eyes quietly, enigmatic and quiet,
one with the flowers' umbels that lean out of the dusk and listen
to something I had on the tip of my tongue but never got said,
something I would not reveal if I could.
And that goes streaming within me in purest joy!

And the flame rises. . . . As if the flowers pressed themselves closer
closer and closer the light in iridescent points.
The aspen quivers and dances, the sunset red strides
and everything that was unspeakable and distant is unspeakable and close.

I sing the only thing that expiates,
the only practical, for all alike.

(translation by Muriel Rukeyser and Leif Sjöberg)

The language and the structure of the poem are important to note.
The language is colloquial, everyday language, but it is rich with realistic nouns. Often Ekelöf may use spoken language; however, it is
usually without the physicality of nouns such as "garden," "notebook,"
"sandwich," "flask," and "pipe." The time of day at first appears
to be night. Later, we learn that there is a streak of "sunset red" still
in the sky. Emphasized in the first stanza are natural and physical
elements immediately in front of the narrator. Writing is a significant

part of these physical phenomena and completely in accord with the other natural actions of eating and drinking.

This description of a concrete world in which the poet seems completely harmonious leads up to the concluding line of the second stanza, "The whole of nature strong in love and death around you." Here, nature's cycle seems to be fully accepted. The third stanza builds outward from this scene and mood. Attempting to convey the singular power of this tranquil moment, the stanza outlines the final evening "before a long, long journey . . ." The unity and naturalness of the experience apparently lead the narrator to some kind of cathartic experience or epiphany in which something that is not or cannot be clearly defined is manifested within the narrator himself.

The comfortable position of the man in "Euphoria," who apparently knows himself and the world around him, is similar to an earlier Ekelöf voyager who seeks a "distant land." The hour of "Euphoria" is just after sunset. In the essay "The Sunset," the narrator as he concludes the essay is comparable to the narrator of this poem. The narrator of "The Sunset" can "breathe out and think about what memories I shall take with me across the sea."

"Euphoria's" narrator is "packed" "before a long, long journey," to the "distant country." The images of distance and "nearness" are explicitly stated, but here instead of being in juxtaposition, as they have been through most of the previous volumes, they are united. The crucial death-in-life theme that has plagued him and presented him with life's meaninglessness and chaos is here comfortably presented "like wine within one."

The final image of the poem has many connotations. Bachelard's theory of substances could be related to the poem, its use of air and fire. Another, and perhaps simpler, approach is to suggest a comparison between this poem and Shakespeare's sonnet 73, "That time of year thou mayst in me behold." One of the more traditional interpretations of this sonnet is that it invokes death in order to heighten the experience of life and love. I suggest absolutely no influence, but feel that perhaps Shakespeare's poem may help the reader to understand Ekelöf's.

The lines that I find open to interpretation in "Euphoria" are those dealing with the fire, "the light's flare that looks me in the eyes . . ."

and "And the flame rises. . . . As if the flowers pressed themselves closer. . . ." The narrator must be looking at a candle or a kerosene lamp, conceivably a star. But how does the rising flame relate to the imagery of the rest of the poem, and how does it lead into the intensity of the closing three lines?

One interpretation might be that a slight wind blows the candle and illuminates the area near the poet, making it seem as if the flowers "pressed themselves closer." The image of the light and the flowers may be combined as they close in upon him in the next line. I find this interpretation somewhat weak. It does not seem to me to lead effectively into the intense purity of the moment indicated by the final line.

Another interpretation, which I suggest as a secondary and far more tentative one but one that provides the depth the moment needs, is related to the subtly pervading awareness of death. Twice mentioned in important lines, death is accepted as part of the poet's vision. The "journey" is probably related to death and some kind of transforming goal, a "distant land."

Shakespeare's imagery in sonnet 73 progresses from autumn to sunset, each of them heading toward their culmination—winter and night. Although I am only concerned with the concluding image of fire, I quote the entire sonnet to give the context of the relevant description.

> That time of year thou mayst in me behold
> When yellow leaves, or none, or few, do hang
> Upon those boughs which shake against the cold,
> Bare ruin'd choirs, where late the sweet birds sang.
> In me thou see'st the twilight of such day
> As after sunset fadeth in the west,
> Which by and by black night doth take away,
> Death's second self, that seals up all in rest.
> In me thou see'st the glowing of such fire
> That on the ashes of his youth doth lie,
> As the death-bed whereon it must expire,
> Consumed with that which it was nourish'd by.
> This thou perceivest, which makes thy love more strong,
> To love that well which thou must leave ere long.

In *Ferry Song*, referring to Charon's ferrying of the dead, "Euphoria" is the concluding poem. This poem finds its narrator tranquil, but intensely aware of both the immediate life around him and the death within it and within himself. He feels this unity like the warmth of wine spreading out through his body. The candle, "the flame rises." Once again death may be making its presence felt, but here in a more subtle form, for as the candle rises it consumes itself, just as the poet's life, even in this moment of profound and heightened beauty, consumes itself. The intensity of the poet's emotion as he realizes this self-destruction, and it may have only flickered at the edge of the poet's consciousness, leads to the apogee of his awareness. As the flame rises, everything around him suddenly takes on a poignant beauty. His new vision of life makes him capable of rising to the beauty of the scene without being frustrated by it. Abruptly, "everything that was unspeakable and distant is unspeakable and close."

Shakespeare's sonnet shows another poet using fire in the same way. Shakespeare's poem intensifies the experience of love. The analogy between an intense moment in one's life and the brief flaring of a candle is easily perceived. For a poet aware of death around him, aware that the candle's flare consumes more rapidly its wick and wax, the pursuit of the analogy between flame and self is easily made. Thus, his own momentary flare, if it does not consume his life more rapidly, makes him "love that well which thou must leave ere long." Such a love may lead to the final harmonious moment of "Euphoria."

The particular recognition of the whole self which both "Open it, Write" and "Euphoria" indicate becomes more apparent in *Non Serviam* (1945), the title of which, according to Ekner, Ekelöf got from James Joyce's *A Portrait of the Artist as a Young Man*.[43] Several of Ekelöf's greatest poems were published in this volume and three of them, "Samothrake," "The Gymnosophist," and "Absentia Animi," give a clear perspective on the mature Ekelöf.

The three poems express interrelated attitudes toward reality and, although they adhere to familiar thematic and imagistic patterns, they extensively expand Ekelöf's poetic range and power. I shall not discuss "Samothrake" in detail as it relates less directly to this study and both Brita Tigerschiöld and Reidar Ekner have commented effectively upon it.

---

[43] Ekner, *I den havandes liv*, p. 27.

The poem "Samothrake" concerns a gigantic ship of death being rowed across what may be infinity to some unknown harbor. Ekner summarizes it in the following way:

> The rowers work steadfastly at their oars and are moved farther and farther back toward the ship's disappearing stern so that continually arriving generations will have a place in the ship's fore, where the goddess of victory shimmers like a galleon's figurehead and image among the clouds, "virgin among storm clouds." All the dead and those yet living have room in the gigantic ship; what the dead have done and have been has not been lost but continues in the living, carries the ship forward in its course.[44]

Significantly, one of the main symbols in "Samothrake" is the "virgin." While she is literally the figurehead on the front of the ship, the virgin's meaning must be related to the "Virgin" of "Open it, Write." She still represents purity, "yet a virgin inviolate advancing ahead of us," and she still remains unattainable and viewing the rowers from an objective position.

Tigerschiöld has pointed out that the theme of the poem, the ship of death, involves both Printz-Påhlson's idea of "a relative certainty of victory," and a "freedom from illusions."[45] Any victory the virgin symbolizes is in some sense related to the acceptance of death, and a complex affirmation of life. It is obvious that the concept of the continuity of time, the continuing relationship between the dead and the living which is metaphorically portrayed in "Samothrake" is related to "Voices."

"The Gymnosophist" expresses philosophically Ekelöf's vision of reality. The poem is essentially conceptual and requires interpretation, since there are few physical facts that can be relied upon for scenery or description. (See p. 144 for poem.) A relatively abstract poem, there is no noun that can be considered a concrete physical reference until the third stanza. The title itself refers to a type of mystic; however, he does not appear until the final lines and then perhaps comically or ironically.

The narrator takes the role of the Gymnosophist and he is trying to define something, "What I mean/what I want." His search is ex-

---

[44] *Ibid.*, p. 55.
[45] Brita Tigerschiöld, "Samothrakes Tema," *BLM* (1959), p. 140.

plicitly related to man's external and internal conditions, neither of
which is adequate. The physical references are not direct. They are
metaphors and similes. It "gets its name when I call." "It is a step
forward before I take it." "It is like the insect the swallow hunts in
the air." Even the narrator remains undefined, difficult to realistically
believe. Is he, like the birds, "standing on one leg in the swamp?"

Explicit statement begins in the fifth stanza, yet it remains difficult
to visualize. "Holy is God Life, holy is God Death." The key subject
of the poem is difficult to define in any terminology. "God Something
Else" is identified by "his halfness," "his half-invisibility," "his turned-
away face." This structure and vocabulary reinforce the substance
of the poem, which is "the greatest secrecy elsewhere preserved."

Ekner has related the poem to Ekelöf's interest in India and suggests
that God Something Else can be identified with India's mystical concept of "nothingness" similar to that of the Taoists. Further, Ekner
suggests a specific statue of Shiva, a four-headed god whose fourth
head is turned away from believers, as the original image that Ekelöf
is describing.[46]

While such a suggestion provides essential background material, it
must be seen in light of Ekelöf's own writing, his many references to
faces, turned away faces, and the positive and negative aspects of
his father—in other words, why the statue fits into Ekelöf's poetic
framework.

The poem fits perfectly into Ekelöf's perspective of his new third
position. The statue must have given him an exciting reinforcement
of his own already established imagery and themes. Naturally, his
interest in mysticism had been growing ever since his interest in art,
so they would seem to be inextricably bound together. We can, of
course, trace "the face" of God Something Else back through "album page," the essays, and "Demon and Angel," and even relate it to the virgin
of "Open it, Write" and "Samothrake." Thus, "God Something Else"
is the newest member of Ekelöf's shadowy mixture of poetic and auto-
biographic personae. Instead of trying to define the exact relationship
between Ekelöf's past and the three present figures, God Fact, God

[46] Ekner, "Herren Någonting Annat—Drömmen om Indien hos Gunnar Ekelöf,"
Ord och Bild (1967), p. 538.

Life, and God Death—all of whom are governed by the powerful God
Something Else—let me suggest a different approach and, hopefully,
throw some additional light on Ekelöf's development.

According to "The Gymnosophist," life and death remain essentially
"unholy" in the light of only "fact." The holiness of life and death
is seen only through "something else." From my initial analysis of
"Voices" to this study, it has been apparent that Ekelöf fits into the
concepts of twentieth-century psychology very well. He uses, often
apparently consciously, material from his own childhood which would
support Freudian interpretations, and one may find in him those cores
of experience common to the subjective experiences of man which
phenomenologists seek to illuminate. But the figure who seems to be
remarkably close to Ekelöf, as Printz-Påhlson has also suggested, is
Carl Gustaf Jung. Jung's work with archetypes and with patients
trying to find a means of creating a whole self, a self that almost tran-
scends the self, may help in evaluating how profound and effective
were the drives and goals of Ekelöf. One statement from Jung gives
an idea of Ekelöf's working within the field of archetypal content.

> What an archetypal content is always expressing is first and foremost a
> "figure of speech." If it speaks of the sun and identifies with it the lion, the
> king, the hoard of gold guarded by the dragon, or the force that makes for
> the life and health of man, it is neither the one thing nor the other, but the
> unknown third thing that finds more or less adequate expression in all these
> similes, yet—to the perpetual vexation of the intellect—remains unknown
> and not to be fitted into a formula.[47]

This "third thing" corresponds very well to the thing that Ekelöf
is trying to define in "The Gymnosophist," and I suspect fits into what
may ultimately begin to be recognized as a pattern in which he seeks
to enter into a dialogue with his unconscious life and to create from
this dialogue, often expressed in archetypal form, substance and content, a whole man. If Ekelöf's extreme poetic drives between what I
have earlier termed transformation and alienation can be put into a
focus whereby the young poet is seen to be seeking personal unity,
his development is evident. In *The Structure and Dynamics of the*

---

[47] Carl Gustaf Jung and C. Kerenyi, *Essays on a Science of Mythology*, trans.
R. F. C. Hull, Bollingen Series 22 (New York, 1949), 105.

Psyche Jung suggests the value of a dialogue between the ego and the unconscious, a process in which the two aspects of the self seem to be in conflict.

> The shuttling to and fro of arguments and affects represents the transcendent function of opposites. The confrontation of the two positions generates a tension charged with energy and creates a living, third thing—not a logical stillbirth in accordance with the principle tertium non datur but a movement out of the suspension between opposites, a living birth that leads to a new level of being, a new situation. The transcendent function manifests itself as a quality of conjoined opposites. So long as these are kept apart—naturally for the purpose of avoiding conflict—they do not function and remain inert.[48]

I propose that the birth of Ekelöf's "something else" fits into his own process of what Jung would call "individuation." The "Virgin" then can be put into a new light. Jung in his description of archetypal content actually refers to a dragon. In various places he suggests that the traditional battle between the hero and the dragon corresponds to the individual's attempt to build his own ego. In "Open it, Write" we read "Life is not the battle of the dragon and the knight, it is the virgin."

Ekner has astutely pointed out that a primary theme of Ekelöf's is his concern with the origins of life, the prenatal world of the womb, and the entire history of an individual which goes back through time up to the union of his parents and finally to the child's own life in the womb and his painful exit from it into life. Jolande Jacobi in explaining Jung's process of individuation says that creation myths "can be understood as symbolical representations of the original coming of consciousness, as its birth so to speak, which happens for the first time in the psyche of the newborn child."[49]

The point of agreement between Ekner and Jung's theories can be focused precisely upon the trio that have been continually developing in Ekelöf's poetry and finally become the dragon, the knight, and the virgin. As there is a parallel between Jung and Ekelöf in terms of the "third thing," there is a remarkably close parallel here too.

[48] Jung, *The Structure and Dynamics of the Psyche*, trans. R. F. C. Hull, Bollingen Series 20 (New York, 1960), p. 90.

[49] Jolande Jacobi, *The Way of Individuation*, trans. R. F. C. Hull (New York, 1967), p. 64.

The central content of the numerous myths in which a dragon or some other monster is dismembered is the acquisition of an independent ego-personality, for which purpose the "devouring, terrible mother" must be overcome. If the individual is to develop and consolidate his ego, the "mother" as the symbol of the darkness of unconsciousness must first be destroyed by the bright light of youthful consciousness, symbolized by the sun's rays or by the arrow, sword, or club. In the second phase of the individuation process it is no longer a question of destruction but of a descent into the dark realm of the unconscious, symbolized by the devouring maw of the death-dealing monster. There in the depths, in the creative womb of the "mother," and with the help of the strong light of consciousness, is found the "treasure hard to attain, ""the precious hoard"—designations for the Self—which the hero must bring back to the light of day.[50]

The insight that this statement gives into "Voices" will become clearer, but for the moment it can be used to bring together my own study, concerned to a large extent with a negative father image that has to be overcome by the poet, and Ekner's study of womb imagery, "Voices," for example shows the "hero" in "the second phase," but failing to bring the "Self" "back to the light of day." The "virgin," although she does have autobiographical, political, and historical associations, is also part of Ekelöf's own ego being born out of the battle of what Sjöberg calls Ekelöf's "antithetical drives."

The poet continues psychologically and poetically to develop through his commitment to writing, and he seeks means by which his maturing "self" can rise even higher or escape its limitations. "The unknown third thing," "God Something Else" is the result of this continuing drive and it allows us some insight into what is often considered one of Ekelöf's most paradoxical qualities: the fact that he is clearly indifferent to Christianity and possibly to most religions; yet he can be considered a mystic, and he uses mystical references throughout much of his later poetry. The answer to the paradox lies in the realization that Ekelöf's mysticism, even if it may be referring in a specific poem to a given Indian statue, is essentially a mysticism of the Self. Exactly how this mysticism functions is illustrated in one of Ekelöf's greatest poems, also published in *Non Serviam*, "Absentia Animi."

[50] *Ibid.*

Before "Absentia Animi," is discussed, however, "The Gymnosophist" should be referred to once again. In terms of the poem itself, it identifies verbally what the narrator "wants," what it is that "God Something Else" can provide. On the first level, "God Something Else" has the capacity to make life and death holy. On a second and more conjectural level, there is the feeling that the narrator would like to escape the circle of life and death, that "Something Else" would allow him to be somewhere else where these limitations do not apply. "And still there is the greatest secrecy elsewhere preserved always elsewhere."

The conclusion of the poem centers in an almost mocking tone upon what I interpret to be the first and highly important level, the perception and experience of the holiness of life. Thus, the "Gymnosophist" stands among images almost always positive for Ekelöf; birds, flowers, and partial light. The final sentence is not a complete one, perhaps an indication of the incompleted search by the Gymnosophist. We note that the birds are not flying.

> Oh heron, oh stork, oh flamingo
> you would-be-wise birds
> standing here around me in the dawn's hour
> among waking flowers
> standing here on one leg in the swamp.

Another element that appears in "The Gymnosophist" and occurs in "Absentia Animi" is a reminiscence of the "dognose" problem. The naming of something denies it the quality of "something else." In a sense this implies a state prior to the correlation of word and reality. That which cannot be read in a line, seen in a face, is that which has power. This hints at one of Ekelöf's most crucial problems, the futility, if not actual philosophical impropriety, of naming anything. His stated theoretical answer to the problem is his "between the lines" theory of poetry mentioned in "An Outsider's Way," a theory that corresponds to Jung's discovery that the unconscious core of experience remains perpetually vexing, that it cannot be fitted into a verbal formula, and that at best one may hint at it in figures of speech, metaphors, and similes common to myth and dream.

A problem related to this theory, and one that may explain some of Ekelöf's attitude toward poetry, is that poetry by becoming poetry gives a thing a form and may inherently lose its potentially transforming quality, the quality of being something else. The dilemma of poetry may be that in its very creation it deprives its creator of the transcending and nameless quality that may have been its source. This potential leads into "Absentia Animi."

Enckell has noted the similarity between "Euphoria" and "Absentia Animi," and points out that whereas "Euphoria" emphasizes the momentary deliverance, "Absentia Animi" succeeds in escaping the limit of the moment.

> The mood over "Absentia Animi" is much darker than the one over "Euphoria" and here there is none of the even breathing of the latter. The light summer-night's idyll is broken and transformed to the raggedness of an autumn landscape with its deserted signs of life and its rotten fertility. The refrain paints the dark: "Meaningless. Unreal. Meaningless." But the poem sends deliverance in a still higher degree than "Euphoria's" "And that goes streaming within me in purest joy!" For that joy still rests in the momentary, while "Absentia Animi" has weeded out the accidental and in the consciousness of death found its resting ground. ... "Absentia Animi" is the alternating song between the two perspectives; the subjective and objective, the non-inverted and the inverted.[51]

Gunilla Bergsten has published a detailed analysis of "Absentia Animi" in a study of the use of Abraxas in Herman Hesse and Gunnar Ekelöf. Part of her analysis hinges upon her disagreement with the generally accepted "darkness" that critics find in the poem.

> This poem is without doubt one of Ekelöf's richest and most beautiful creations. At the same time that its soft sounds rock one to rest, it awakens and disturbs by its mysteriousness. It offers the purest word music but also a magical semantic. The mysteriousness and the magic are concentrated in the "Abraxas," whose rich sound effects Ekelöf exploits in a sovereign play.[52]

She continues her study by giving the meaning and origin of "abraxas," a cabbalist and gnostic word used in place of the name of Jehovah or Mithras, since these names were sacred and could not be spoken. She points out that most Swedish critics have interpreted the word to be "meaninglessness" or nonsense. The emphasis upon "meaning-

[51] Enckell, "Det omvända perspektivet," *Prisma* (1950), p. 26.

[52] Gunilla Bergsten, "Abraxas. Gunnar Ekelöf: Absentia Animi," *Svenska Diktanalyser* (Stockholm, 1965), p. 199, and "Abraxas: Ett motiv hos Herman Hesse och Gunnar Ekelöf," *Samlaren* (1964).

lessness" she agrees is significant and quotes Ekelöf's own comment from "An Outsider's Way" "that meaninglessness gives life its meaning," but she feels the poem definitely does not stop with this mood. (See p. 146 for poem.)

"The Gymnosophist" had established "something else" that has power over life and death. The contrast of the "meaninglessness" of the early part of "Absentia Animi" and the mysticism of the latter half becomes clear in the phrase translated into English as "thesis antithesis synthesis." In the last half of the poem Bergsten feels there is a change.

> But here the word "synthesis" has fallen away; with a leap we leave the polar sea of logical thought and are carried up to the level of the incomprehensible and unnameable. "Thesis antithesis abrasax" followed by "You also I" the union of opposites, the integration of object and subject.[53]

The theme of "something else" becomes predominant at this point. Similar to "God Something Else" this theme cannot be defined in words or pictures, an example, according to Bergsten, of the mystical "via negativa," the method of defining a thing by defining what it is not.

> Abraxas—or abrasax—thus, stands in "Absentia Animi" as symbol for the empty meaningless rustling and prattling with words and meanings which disintegrate into unreality, but within this meaningless unreality Something Else conceals itself, that which cannot be expressed in words but which is more real than everything that can be expressed in words.[54]

She admits that the conclusion returns to a hopeless emptiness, but she feels this represents the everyday, rational life. There are, however, moments when that everyday nonsense can be transformed into abraxas.

> At the poem's conclusion we are again back down on the earth, on the ground. Everything is as it was before, but not exactly, for something has happened in between. But it is like a dream.[55]

The title of the poem Bergsten interprets to mean absence from self, distraction, and the mystic's apparent unawareness which is in fact an inner concentration. It seems to me that in light of its imagery something more may be said of the poem. The juxtaposition of the

---

[53] Bergsten, *Svenska Diktanalyser*, p. 207.
[54] *Ibid.*, p. 209.
[55] *Ibid.*, p. 210.

titles of "The Gymnosophist" and "Absentia Animi" again indicates
something. "The Gymnosophist" is basically a persona who is present
talking about that which is not present. "Absentia Animi" reverses
this process by indicating an absence and relating it to that which
is present. Precisely how this development occurs may be observed
in closer detail.

The structure of "Absentia Animi" follows Ekelöf's more common
pattern. It begins with a specific scene, progresses from the scene to
thoughts about his writing, then leads to identification with an object
in the scene and thoughts from its perspective, and finally back through
the narrator's own thoughts to the scene itself.

The narrator sees the autumn scene outside, is aware of night sinking
down, and hears the cicadas. The sound stimulates his own creative
imagination, if we may differentiate that for the moment from his
intellectual response to the scene, and he thinks of his own writing.
"My poem rustles Words do their work and lie there . . ." ". . . the
meaning with the rustling is the rustling." Words cannot equal reality.
He returns again to the specific scene and sees the bird, "an overlooked
blackbird sings in a treetop for nothing, for the throat's sake." (Bergsten
points out the connection between the god "abraxas" and bird symbols
of him as well as the potential of a symbolic "rebirth" connected to
these symbols, yet she draws no connection between the bird and
abraxas in Ekelöf's poem. It can be suspected that Ekelöf consciously
used the bird as a traditional symbolic representation of "abraxas.")
The narrator imagines himself to be the bird, apparently complete and
self-contained, yet finds "I wish nothing more I wish myself far far
away." The bird reenacts the narrator's situation.

> O deep down in me
> in that which is near
> is something beyond
> something beyond-near
> in what is near and far
> something neither nor
> in what is either-or:

The circle of magic "non sens," the final closing scene in which
"spiders spin their webs across the silent night / cicadas scrape / In
autumn," all of these lead to "something else," if the reader looks for

it. To interpret the closing scene at face value by "meaningless," "unreal," or whatever, may be to deny the poet part of his poem. On one level it is possible that the final lines are presented *because* the narrator is looking beyond them at "something else." He does not fall back, nor has the experience been momentary. The poem has been an "absence" trying to define itself in terms of "presence." In this sense it is a reversal of Ekelöf's traditional technique. In terms of its content and imagery, however, it is consistent with his development, with his process of negative affirmation, whether it is called "evolutionary primitivism" or a definition of optimism defined in terms of skepticism.

The poem has acted out its own concept, for the narrator has in fact sought "something else" in the scene before his eyes. We know this because the scene opens the poem, and he goes beyond it in order to see it in relation to "something else." He has found "something else," just as the poem indicates: he found it partially in the bird, partially "deep down" in himself, and partially in the statement and action of the poem. In the most extreme and paradoxical terms, however, he finds it by not finding it. "Words do their work," but they go elsewhere. "He who partout seeks the meaning of all things has long since realized that the meaning with the rustling is the rustling." The words must go elsewhere if he is to enact his statement. The scene itself remains, but one feels that as long as anyone is capable of looking into that scene, he is capable of finding "something else" there. The clue that is so important to the discovery of this circular process is the title "Absentia Animi" which I feel emphasizes the discovery of self, and possibly the rising above self, by absence from the self. This, of course, fits within a variety of mystical traditions from Zen Buddhism to Gnosticism.

We may look at the poem in light of the poet, however, and find another means, a second level, of perceiving the poem's concern with the wholeness of the self. Ekelöf is consistently involved with the problem of opposites, and in some ways the progression of his first twenty years of writing concerns the attempt at uniting into a self the fragmented opposites that he finds within himself and were cultivated by his ambivalent childhood. Bergsten touches upon this "union of opposites," but Jung in *Psychology and Alchemy* suggests a definition of the self which exactly and almost word for word parallels Ekelöf's theme in this poem, a theme crucial to this part of his life.

> The self is a union of opposites par excellence, and this is where it differs essentially from the Christian symbol. The androgyny of Christ is the utmost concession the Church has made to the problem of opposites. The opposition between light and good on the one hand and darkness and evil on the other is left in a state of open conflict, since Christ simply represents good, and his counterpart the devil, evil. This opposition is the real world problem which is still unsolved at present. The self, however, is absolutely paradoxical in that it represents in every respect thesis and antithesis, and at the same time synthesis.[56]

The German original uses the same words "Thesis und Antithesis und zugleich Synthesis darstellt." The Swedish uses "sats motsats slutsats abrasax abraxas Sats." While the English and German parallel make the similarity seem exact when it is not, the translation seems to me to be an accurate and logical one. What such a parallel suggests, assuming there is no direct influence though there is little doubt that Ekelöf was aware of contemporary psychology and psychoanalysis, is that the mysticism, the "something else" with which Ekelöf is concerned, is an inner one, one in which the self becomes Self ("Sats" is capitalized), a point comparable to the Eastern sense of "enlightened" and, thus, "absentia animi," freed from, beyond awareness of self, or totally one's self to a degree that one loses "self consciousness."

I am not suggesting that Ekelöf reached a point of enlightenment at this stage of his life, nor that he necessarily realized in the Jungian tradition the "whole Self" which would give his life a constant unity and power such as those moments suggested in "Euphoria" and enacted in a much more profound way in terms of its union of opposites in "Absentia Animi," but I do feel there is enough evidence to indicate that he was probing with remarkable clarity and consciousness the depths of his being, the conscious and unconscious parts of his life, in order to gain the tranquillity and dominion of self that he felt he should attain in his life.

One of the ways by which man can put himself in touch with his own unconscious depths is by invoking indirectly what cannot be reached

---

[56] Jung, *Psychology and Alchemy*, no. 12, p. 19.

by direct invocation. The poem may well be offering to both reader and poet a means of "reading between the lines," a method of looking beyond the scene to "something else." As Bergsten has so clearly shown, "abraxas" is crucial to the poem's meaning. Reduced to an extreme simplification, the phrase "In autumn" which concludes the poem may be its own kind of "abraxas," as is to some degree the poem as a whole, an indirect invocation of the Self.

One cannot help but be impressed by the weight of meaning placed upon the phrase "In autumn" by the fact that the title of Ekelöf's next book is *In Autumn* (1951). This collection of poems with its assembled pieces from the past contains the poem that began this study. We may now see "Voices" with a somewhat richer sense both of its context and of its meaning. The first poem in *In Autumn*, "A Reality (dreamed)" begins with a negation, "I do not believe in a life after this," and offers "a feeling of happiness which comes seldom but comes anyway," and concludes with these three lines:

> Fleeting is all consciousness,
> but fleeting is not futile.
> Thus finishes my bucolic song.

Perhaps not the lines of an enlightened man, but certainly lines by a man who is seeking and occasionally finding an inner and / or whole self. The poem seems to suggest that reality is an old fence, fallen leaves, a sunset with a degree of freedom and happiness to be found primarily within the realm of one's own consciousness.

How then does "Voices Under the Ground" fit into this perspective of a man who is finding self-acceptance, and who, in moments of writing or in experiences of nature, sometimes realizes the highest conscious-ness of self? Although "Voices" follows Ekelöf's traditional pattern of beginning with a scene, responding to it in his thought, identifying with it, then returning to the scene, it is a dark and brooding poem seemingly ending in a checkmate between the womb of devouring darkness and the figure of death, or between consciousness and un-consciousness. The poem, with its archetypal content, seen in the context of the poet's life, is an attempt to enter into dialogue with the grumbling pit of the unconscious. Freud and Jung have indicated how important it is to give vent to the unconscious, but how to do it is always an individual and often difficult task. Jung offers a description of one way in *The Structure and Dynamics of the Psyche.*

> The way this can be done is best shown by those cases in which the "other" voice is more or less distinctly heard. For such people it is technically simple to note down the "other" voice in writing and to answer its statement from the standpoint of the ego. It is exactly as if a dialogue were taking place between two human beings with equal rights, each of whom gives the other credit for a valid argument and considers it worth while to modify the conflicting standpoints by means of thorough comparison and discussion or else to distinguish them clearly from one another. Since the way to agreement seldom stands open, in most cases a long conflict will have to be borne, demanding sacrifices from both sides.[57]

Jung's description suggests the possibility that "Voices" represents part of the argument that is overheard during a conflict. Nevertheless, it is from this type of confrontation that the "third thing" is born. While no rebirth may occur within this poem, the fact that the poem exists and that it is a part of a large number of poems verifies that we are being shown one of the introverted and more painful moments of a dialogue that is productive.

Because of the very nature of "Voices," interpretation of it still remains open. I have indicated various ranges within it and suggested realms of experience upon which it touches, but I am incapable of believing that this poem, similar to others by Ekelöf such as "Absentia Animi" or much of his later poetry, is fully analyzed or is capable of being limited to a precise interpretation.

I do feel that much of Ekelöf's poetry becomes more meaningful when read within the psychological and critical frameworks that I have suggested. A poem like "Open it, Write" for instance when read with Jung's writings in mind is even more powerful, and I think I have established how effectively Bachelard's theories apply to "Voices Under the Ground." Few poets have used so profoundly the borderline of consciousness to explore and to define poetically what we might think of as the "abraxas" of the self.

Elizabeth Sewell's book *The Orphic Voice*[58] offers a tradition much older than our own century in which one might place Ekelöf, almost

---

[57] Jung, *The Structure and Dynamic of the Psyche*, no. 8, p. 88.
[58] Elizabeth Sewell, *The Orphic Voice* (New Haven, 1960).

in spite of his aversion to the traditional concept of God. This tradition includes, among others, Linnaeus, Wordsworth, and Rilke. It basically represents the conscious poetic and intellectual tradition of self-awareness in relation to language, and the attempt at reading the hieroglyphics of the mysterious universe. "Absentia Animi" may fit into this tradition where the universe is not decoded on the assumption that it is an inanimate object that can be definitively analyzed but rather an attempt is made to interpret the provocative and organic symbols of nature. These symbols in turn continuously give new interpretations to man of himself.

In a book about the turn of the century Swedish poet Vilhelm Ekelund, Carl-Erik af Geijerstam makes a statement about the nature of the paradox in general which I feel serves as a good comment about the poetry of Gunnar Ekelöf.

> The true paradox—the one which aims further than a verbal game—wants to convey a new understanding or a new discovery of something sunken. The existence of this other world is given through the contradictions in the world where one is. In such a paradox there is often a word with a negative content .... It is the negative which is the paradox's center, for there is where the transformation arises. Through knowing "want" one can reach over to a world where other measurements hold.

> An aphorism by Valery expresses precisely this way forward through a need revealed: "I am worth something through that which I lack." In the same way but still stronger is Monsieur Teste's utterance on the world of the senses as a hindrance to experience: "What I see makes me blind." The closing word blind opens the possibility of transformation: one suspects the nearness of a world where blindness ceases. Through destroying the positive and replacing it with a negative the movement does not stop. One stands at a beginning—still blind but with the possibility of sight. Goethe's relinquishment and continuance idea such as it is expressed in the words stirb und werde is near to this. That the continuance idea was clear to Valery is apparent if one cites further in his text: "This field of light before me is a blindfold over the eyes and hides either a darkness or another light, something more."[59]

In conclusion, "Voices Under the Ground" gives a perspective on Ekelöf's development. Within this poem may be heard echoes of the twenty-year search that he undertook in order to enter into and express the dialogue that may begin in the mind, but reaches the un-

---

[59] Carl Erik af Geijerstam, *Det Personliga Experimentet* (Stockholm, 1963), p. 110.

conscious life of man. The result of the search and the dialogue, neither of which ever really ceased during his life, was a paradoxical Self founded upon a childhood grounded in the concepts of "meaningless-ness" and "death-in-life." The themes and images that are here recur in Ekelöf's later work. The reader's obligation remains the same: to see specifically what the lines say in order to read, as Ekelöf suggests in "An Outsider's Way," "*between* the words, *between* the lines, *between* the meanings."

POEMS AND PROSE BY EKELÖF

Written Down in 1932

1

Trivial facts
I do not sleep at night I cannot sleep I do not even think I want to
I wake in the mornings without noticing it
I have no refuge in sleep or truth my dreams are extinguished my everything
    is gone my universe one and the same
I have desires only in my pains but I must deny myself even in the depth
    of my dreams
I write badly my doubt is too great to have room in words
I have suicidal dark flashes
As when someone feels a nerve stitch through the body so I feel too often
    to live
I cannot lose renounce deny my self
I dare not lose renounce deny my other self
my foundation and my end

2

Forgive me if I write badly
Forgive me if I write stupidly
It is late or early for different people
It is late or early for different lights
The shellfish have gone into hibernation
The fish have eaten their pearls in order to sleep
Sleep is a precious present costly values sleep sends
The clock wakes up daily and twists the beach a circle toward the sun
I am tired to death as never years or days
It sinks it sinks the evening cloud's gloria no clouds
I love the sunken as myself all presence is too strong
I was alone in the puzzle
Rest in each other or rest in your self
And why should it be so difficult to end
Why should life be so careless
Hands cut off no one may come up in the lifeboat to the dawn
No one may come up
but why should it be so difficult to end
or to adapt
or to break the habit
I give up myself now as I gave myself away
Nightlessness defeats me

[115]

The morning light's gray wings force me to flee
From loneliness's depth comes cry after cry
from solitude's saltsea unreality
I long from the red thread
to the blue
I drive my madness aside to the room's corners
I am colorless and dawnbitter
The cruelty everyone's cruelty rips apart my doubt and the day breaks
    through
Perhaps my blood is white

3

In stillness the morning light crushes the drug of sleep
in stillness stonelight tombstone urinelight the memories of sickness
I fondled a stone, it was closed and dreamed alone
Perhaps there were petrified birds in there
In thousandyear beats beat my stone heart in my veins
Time glided beneath my feet, before I knew it I was gone
How could I see how I should adapt to death in life
In a different light the stone became a living bird and flew away
The area empty and the heart full
Everything turned in me everything flew away
The bird took my wings and gave them to another light
It was dark around me
I groped around and got nothing in my hands
no one to look for with my hands empty stones nothing to fondle
and nothing to forget
The only way to forget is the light of the abyss
On the bottom of the abyss no one can forget, there is no rope to lift oneself
    up to the light of the abyss
The house of the stars is empty and all the sisters are away with each other
The limestone walks alone on the bottom and shines among the fish
Mute, dumb they waver about in their own light
I have no one else's light
I cannot close my eyes over anyone else's luck
I cannot sleep in my own
The house of the abyss is forgetfulness not one's own but others'
This is hell
And all these invalids who wander homeless through the wards have only
    walls for doctors
Lines of the temperature chart climb the closed doors
Everything lies on its back
Everyone's eyes are open and empty.

4

I am sick and the world churns my soul to death
My feet take hold on the pavingstones and squalor
No lampdreams scatter the slums' need
No waterdrops sizzle to steam on the thirsting man's hot lips
Rain
Rain for eternity amen
Rain over clasped hands and newly-combed hair
Rain which sinks down in death's dirt
Autumn rain
Autumn for eternity amen
Autumn with icecold skies and the leaning of melancholy thoughts
Autumn over the canal's leafless branches clay green ponds
Late autumn
Late on the earth for eternity amen
Late on the earth when the clock stops falling and the bed stops creaking
It is eight years later now and nothing has gotten better
All the earth's stones are sleepy the granite dreams good dreams
the gneiss bad
The lamps stare hard at the slums' need
My feet take hold on the eternal staircase
The spiral twists dizzying in the intestine's whispering
Sick is my soul and the world turns my watch to death's
The world turns time slowly and feelinglessly around its axis
Staryear after staryear the stars fall
like snow on everything.

5

I thread the heavy words, coalpearls on the strings
I think slowly without precision without any other will than movement
In life's cosmic process I have always reacted against the noble metals
in life's legal process I have lost my I
Now it is time to spell and put together
to think slowly choose equally heavy and uniform words
fabricate ugly necklaces to exchange for noble metals for heathens
time to react to change slowly and noticeably
to another than myself
Night rests heavy and dark against the windowpanes
What tremendous pressure against the windowpanes on the ground floor
If one opened a window night would rush in
fill the floor with darkness rise from floor to floor like water
The wind rushes around the gables of the house

It throbs in the radiators and the lamps' light offers opposition
A white loneliness against a black loneliness
Why not mix everything light and energy to a uniform consistence
Life divides and sorts. Life passes death by
Poor and deserted loves
Death was passed by whenever there were promotions
Death stayed sitting there like some wretched employee

A Deathdream

I seemed to fondle a stone with my hand.
Perhaps there were petrified birds and flowers in there.
With thousand year beats beat my stone heart in my veins.
In my hand the stone became a living bird and flew away.
I stood there alone. My bird is gone
but comes back sometimes out of habit or duty.
It chirps miserably. It leaves me again.
It chirps about its life, wants to fly, has already flown.
(A diplomatic fight for freedom!)
Myself being bound to the stone, the primal stone.
I fondled a stone, I became a stone.
All things turned in me, everything was transformed.
Now time turns slowly and feelinglessly around its axis.
My feet take hold on the feelingless spiral
the stone staircase turning in dizziness like a wide-eyed dream
from landing to landing, from step to step of stone.
I take them one after one, and my head turns.
I smother in stone, I drown in stone.
Around me sleep birds and shellfish
among lizards and flowers.
In thousand year beats beat their hearts of stone
in veins of stone.
They breathe regularly in stone
on pillows of stone, under sheets of stone.
In yearbillions time draws them with itself
through seas of stone, to heavens of stone . . .

—Where am I? Where am I? Wake up!
All the more and more distant the cry is heard:
—Where am I? Wake up!

Röster Under Jorden

Timmarna går. Tiden förgår.
Det är sent eller tidigt för olika mänskor
Det är sent eller tidigt för olika ljus.

—Stilla stöter morgonljuset sömnens drog
och gömmer undan den i alla apotek
(med de svart-vit-rutiga golven)—
färglös och gryningsbitter
själv trött som aldrig år och dagar intill döden . . .
—Jag längtar från den svarta rutan till den vita.
—Jag längtar från den röda tråden till den blå.
Den där unge mannen! (det är något fel med hans ansikte)—
Den där bleka flickan! (hennes hand är hos blommorna i fönstret:
hon existerar bara i samband med sin hand
som bara existerar i samband med . . .)
Fågeln som flyger och flyger. Med sin flykt.
Någon som gömmer sig. Andra som bara finns i samband med annat.
Gumman som smyger och smyger tills hon blir upptäckt.
Då vänder hon sig listigt leende och retirerar.
Men hom kommer tillbaka.
Vaktmästaren vid pulpeten (målad i genomnött furuådring). Han har inga
ögon.
Barnet vänt mot den svarta tavlan, alltid vänt emot tavlan.
Pekpinnens gnissel. Var är handen?
Den finns hos blommorna i fönstret.
Lukten av krita. Vad säger oss lukten av krita?
Att timmarna går, tiden förgår.
Att sakta pulvriserar morgonljuset sömnens drog . . .
. . . med de svart-vit-rutiga golven—

Archaeopteryx! Vilket vackert namn!
Archaeopteryx! Min fågel!
—Varför kvittrar den så olyckligt?
—Den kvittrar om sitt liv, vill flyga bort, har kanske redan flugit.
Jag smekte den redan som sten.
Med tusenåriga slag slog mitt stenhjärta i ådrorna.
Kanske fanns det förstenade fåglar och ödlor därinne!
Rhamphornycus! Archaeopteryx!
I ett nytt ljus blev stenen levande fågel och flög sin kos
men kommer ibland av plikt eller vana tillbaka.
Alltid blir någon liggande kvar, det är det hemska.
—Iguanodon!

Voices Under the Ground

Hours pass. Time passes by.
It is late or early to different people.
It is late or early by different light.
—Silently, the morning light shrugs away the drug of sleep
and hides it in all the pharmacies
(with black-white checkered tile floors)—
colorless and dawnbitter
tired as never years and days to death . . .
—I long from the black square to the white.
—I long from the red thread to the blue.

That young man! (there is something wrong with his face)—
That pale girl! (her hand is in the flowers at the window:
she exists only in connection with her hand
which exists only in connection with . . .)
The bird that flies and flies. With its flight.
Someone hides. Others who exist only in relation to something else.
The old woman who sneaks and sneaks until she is discovered.
Then she turns slyly smiling and retires.
But she comes back.
The caretaker at the desk (painted in well-worn pinegrain). He has no eyes.
The child turned toward the blackboard, always turned to the blackboard.
The pointer's screech. Where is the hand?
It is in the flowers at the window.
The smell of chalk. What does the smell of chalk tell us?
That hours pass, time passes by.
That slowly morning light pulverizes the drug of sleep . . .
. . . with the black-white checkered floors . . .

Archaeopteryx! What a lovely name!
Archaeopteryx! My bird!
—Why does it chirp so unhappily?
—It chirps about its life, wants to fly away, has already flown perhaps.
I fondled it already as a stone.
With thousand-year beats beat my stoneheart in my veins.
Perhaps there were petrified birds and lizards in there.
Rhamphornycus! Archaeopteryx!
In a new light the stone became a living bird and flew away
but sometimes either from habit or duty comes back.
Someone is always left behind, that is the horror.
—Iguanodon!

[121]

Fågeln är borta men säger sig vara kvar—är det för att skydda sig?
Hur skulle den vara kvar? Den är inte kvar. Det är du som är kvar.
Fågeln är fri. Det är du som väntar.
Jag väntar.
Jag längtar till fågeln som flyger och flyger
med sin flykt.
Själv blev jag bunden vid stenen, den forna stenen.
Sista tiden har fågeln klagat på att den inte kan sova.
Vem kan sova?
Jag väckte fågeln en natt—den var hemma.
Jag väckte den därför att mina tankar plågade mig.
Jag ville veta.
Fågeln säger sig flyga bort för att kunna göra mig så mycket större glädje—
En diplomatisk frihetskamp!
Jag smekte en sten, jag blev en sten.
Jag blev sista biten i puzzlespelet
biten som ingenstans passar, bilden hel mig förutan.
Alltid blir någonting över, det är det hemska.
Allting vände sig i mig, allting förflyktigades.
Fågeln tog mina vingar och skänkte dem åt ett annat ljus.
Det släcktes. Det blev mörkt.
Archaeopteryx! Archaeopteryx!
Jag trevade omkring mig, fick ingenting i händerna
ingenting att minnas, ingenting att glömma . . .

—Finns ingen glömska i avgrundens hus?
—Inte när allt är avgrund.
—Finns inget ljus?
—Inte när det är släckt.
—Är der dag eller natt?
—Det är natt.
—Vad lyktorna stirrar hårt!
—De håller vakt över stenarna.
—Så långt under ytan?
—Det finns ingen yta!
Men där, på bottnen, ser jag en ensam kalksten bland fiskarna . . .

Stumma, döva strövar de kring i sitt eget ljus.
Den har inget ljus.
Den har ingen botten.
Den kan inte sluta sina ögon över någons lycka.
Den kan inte öppna dem.
—Detta är helvetet!
—Nej, det är tomhet.
Och stjärnonas hus är tomt
och själarna

The bird is gone but says it is still there—is that to protect itself?
How can it still be there? It is not there. It is you who are left there.
The bird is free. It is you who wait.
I wait.
I long for the bird which flies and flies
with its flight.
I myself am bound to the stone, the primal stone.
Lately the bird has complained that it cannot sleep.
Who can sleep?
I woke the bird one night—it was at home.
I woke it because my thoughts plagued me.
I wanted to know.
The bird says it flies away to give me a much greater happiness—
A diplomatic fight for freedom!
I fondled a stone, I became a stone.
I was the last piece in the puzzle
the piece which fit nowhere, kept out by the picture.
Something is always left over, that is the horror.
Everything twisted in me, everything turned to vapor.
The bird took my wings and gave them to another light.
The light went out. It was dark.
Archaeopteryx! Archaeopteryx!
I groped around, got nothing in my hands
nothing to remember, nothing to forget . . .

—Is there no forgetfulness in the house of the abyss?
—Not when everything is abyss.
—Is there no light?
—Not when it is out.
—Is it day or night?
—It is night.
—How hard the lamps stare!
—They watch over the stones.
—So far beneath the surface!
—There is no surface.
But there on the bottom, I see a single limestone among the fish . . .
Dumb, deaf they wander in their own light.
It has no light.
It has no bottom.
It cannot close its eyes over someone's joy.
It cannot open them.
—This is hell!
—No, it is emptiness.
And the house of the stars is empty
and the souls

drar bort ur universum—
Jorden lindar sakta och känslolös tiden kring sin axel,
mer uttänjbar än något gummiband.
Fötterna måste ta spjärn i den ändlöst vindlande spiraltrappan,
trappspindeln som vrider sig svindlande likt en storögd dröm
från avsats till avsats, i trappsteg på trappsteg av sten . . .

Du håller huvudet stilla:
Du tvingas ta trappstegen ett efter ett och kroppen vrider sig:
Du vrider huvudet av dig.
Du kvävs i sten, du svävar i trögflytande sten, du sover därinne.
Fåglar och snäckor sover därinne som du
med ödlor och blommor,
till och med regndroppar sover
på kuddar av sten, under lakan av sten.
Med tusenåriga slag slår deras hjärtan av sten
i ådror av sten.
I årbillioner av sten virvlar tiden dem med sig
i rasande stormar av sten genom hav av sten
till himlar av sten . . .

—Vär är jag? Var är du?
—Vakna!
—Var är jag?
—I avgrundens hus.
—Finns ingen glömska i avgrundens hus?
—Inte ens egen men andras.
Och alla dessa sjuklingar som driver hemlösa runt salarna
har bara väggarna till läkare.
Feberkurvorna stapplar härs och tvärs över de tillbommade dörrarna.
Allting ligger på rygg, allting vänder sig
ständigt och ständigt på rygg. Man vet inte
vad som är upp eller ner. Allting vänder sig
ständigt och ständigt på rygg,
till och med stolarna, till och med väggar och golv.
Allt vänder sig.
Allas ögon är blanka och tomma som fönstren,
man ser inte natt eller dag . . .

—Är det natt eller dag?
—Det är natt
och natten vilar speglande och svart mot fönsterrutorna.
Natten stiger, natten är snart vid fjärde våningen.
Natten är snart vid femte våningen.
Natten är snart vid sjätte våningen.
Nu är natten vid sjunde våningen.

draw away from the universe—
The earth winds, slowly and feelinglessly, time around its axis,
more pliable than a rubber band.
The feet must step on the stairs of the endlessly winding spiral staircase,
the stair spindle twisting dizzily as a wide-eyed dream

from landing to landing, on stair after stair of stone . . .
You hold your head still:
You are forced to take the stairs one after another and your body twists:
Your head twists.
You suffocate in stone, you choke in sluggish stone, you sleep there.
Birds and shellfish sleep there like you
with lizards and flowers,
even raindrops sleep
on pillows of stone, under sheets of stone.
With thousand-year beats beat their hearts of stone
in veins of stone.
For yearbillions of stone time swirls them with itself
in raging storms of stone through seas of stone
to heavens of stone . . .

—Where am I? Where are you?
—Wake up!
—Where am I?
—In the house of the abyss.
—Is there no forgetfulness in the house of the abyss?
—Not one's own but others'.
And all these invalids who drift homeless around the rooms
have only walls for doctors.
Temperature charts stumble at random on the blockaded doors.
Everything lies on its back, everything turns
again and again on its back. One does not know
what is up or down. Everything turns
again and again on its back,
even the chairs, even walls and floors.
Everything turns.
Everyone's eyes are blank and empty as windows,
one does not see night or day . . .

—Is it night or day?
—It is night
and the night rests, a mirror, black against the windowpanes.
The night rises, the night is soon at the fourth floor.
The night is soon at the fifth floor.
The night is soon at the sixth floor.
Now the night is at the seventh floor.

—Hur många våningar finns det?
—Många.
—Vilket oerhört tryck mot rutorna i bottenvåningen!
Sprängdes de skulle natten forsa in,
fylla golven med mörker, stiga från våning till våning!
—Undan däruppe i trappan!
—Trängs lagom!
—Snubbla på bara!
Det dunkar i värmeledningen som i ett ansträngt hjärta,
det blinkar dött i lamporna när de presterar mottryck
och söker hålla mörkret nere
En vit ensamhet mot en svart ensamhet.
Eller en svart ensamhet mot en vit ensamhet.
Och medan mörkret forsar omkring husets gavlar
kommer ur alla dessa ensamheter rop på rop av tystnad:
—Vem är du, skugga vid den furumålade pulpeten,
fläckad av skolbläck, ristad med pennknivar
genom de många generationernas lager av påmålningar?
—Döden blev förbigången vid alla befordringar.
Döden blev sittande på sin plats som en usel vaktmästare.

Timmarna går. Tiden förgår.
Sakta pulvriserar morgonljuset sömnens drog.
—Jag längtar från den svarta rutan till den vita.
—Jag längtar från den röda tråden till den blå.

—How many floors are there?
—Many.
—What a tremendous pressure against the windowpanes on the groundfloor.
If they shattered night would rush in,
fill the rooms with darkness, rise from floor to floor!
—Rapidly, up there in the staircase!
—There's enough pushing!
—Better step on it!
It throbs in the radiators like a strained heart,
the lamps blink dead when they offer opposition
and try to hold back the darkness.
A white loneliness against a black loneliness.
Or a black loneliness against a white loneliness.
And while the darkness rushes around the gables of the house
from all of these lonelinesses come cry after cry of silence:
—Who are you, shadow at the painted-pine desk,
flecked with school ink, carved by penknives
through many generations of repainted surfaces?
—Death was bypassed at all the promotions.
Death was left sitting in his place like a useless caretaker.

Hours pass. Time passes by.
Slowly the morning light pulverizes the drug of sleep.
—I long from the black square to the white.
—I long from the red thread to the blue.

A Photograph

On the table in front of me I have a photograph that I shall attempt to describe as thoroughly as possible. It portrays a room, a salon. In the middle at the back stands one half of a double door partially open. To the left of the door, above the light switch, is the room thermometer, important, because the apartment was still heated with a porcelain Dutch-oven. Around the room runs a medium high 18th century style panel; on the floor lies a passively restful Turkish carpet; high up shimmers a glimpse of a crystal chandelier.

To the right of the half-open door one sees a living room sofa-set with gilted, late Gustavian furniture covered with thin-striped embroidered material: a sofa, a table, two armchairs and two chairs. The table has one green-veined panel going upward with a black one just like it going downward; the legs are bent and cross over one another like eights, sawed off at the bottom and the top. On the edges under the table-top are decorated carvings, something reminiscent of the style Masreliez took home with him. Even the sofa has a little Pompeian line. On the table's corner stands a flower, a cyclamen or perhaps a little azalea, and because of this my guess is that it is late winter, a guess for which the tentative, cloudy light in the room also speaks. The photographer stood with his back facing the two windows opening out to the street.

Above the sofa hang five pictures: a woman's portrait from the same time as the furniture and grouped around her four color-tinted copperplate engravings from the story of Achilles, of which I especially remember the one where Achilles clothes himself as a girl with distaff in hand in order to escape going to the Trojan war, to which a squatting messenger with tucked-up robe (Odysseus) invites him.

Visible in the far left corner of the photograph is a glimpse of a lamp-bracketed mirror on the far wall, and of a pianoforte with its keyboard turned toward the window.

All of these objects are, however, only silent witnesses, motionless partners to the similarly motionless person who "populates" the picture. He sits in a lovely rococo armchair, for safety's sake on a pile of blankets, turned toward the light and with his feet on a matching stuffed hassock so that one sees little of the soles of the heavy shoes over the hassock's edge. The long legs are dressed in gray-striped pants; he has his hands in his lap. The coat is black and can be a formal jacket; the shirt front is starched and white, the collar conventional with two tips and supplied with a black bow. Apart from the bow-tie one can say that he has on a traditional English banker's suit. Between the collar and the chin a clean white handkerchief is tucked; perhaps he cut himself when he was shaved in the morning. But what gives the entire picture its unique life, or lack of life, is the long taut oval face. The forehead is high; the eyebrows moderately protruding; the nose short and straight and the chin strong. The corners of the mouth are slanted down and the moustaches seem

[128]

to hang down loosely. The eyes look toward the photographer but there is
no glance in them, or how shall I say it: they follow only mechanically and
automatically the photographer's proceedings with his box, just as the eyes
are accustomed to even if their owner is absent and far away in other thoughts.
The person in the armchair, however, has no thoughts, or if he has some they
are extraordinarily fragmentary and subhuman.   Inside the high forehead
he owns a swarming coral reef. Nature will think hereafter for him, if an abstraction such as "nature" can think, or if a coral reef can think. The expression
on his face I cannot describe other than by exclusions. It is not a dead man's
face, not a living man's either. It has nothing animalish, but if it has on the
other side something human, it gives the human a kind of transparent impression. I nearly said that there was something gloomily vegetating in it,
but of the gloom one cannot speak for the expression is far beyond that and
all other emotions, and not of the vegetating for it is nearer something lifeless.
It is in itself a work so far beyond all adjectives and attempts at descriptions
that one finally has only the word "terrible" left. Anyway the face is not
inhuman, but it forces one to revise his idea of what "terrible" is. It is the
meaningless.

I just mentioned the handkerchief between the collar and the cheek and
it strikes me how well attended he was every day. During all those years I
never came to think of the barber who came every morning, and I wonder just
how he considered his job of regularly shaving that visage. It is certain that
he was well paid, however. What was generally thought I could hear one day
in a conversation between two nurses. There was one day, a spring day, when
he was neither apathetic nor restless but somewhere between: for this reason
he was dressed in overcoat and bowler, got his walking stick in his hand and
was taken out for a promenade with a nurse on each side. This, combined with
spring, seemed to me very grand and promising, and I followed behind in their
wake. When the trio came to the corner of St. John's Street and Jutas Hill
there was a little fidgeting, but not much. He absolutely wanted to take the
steep stairway—they were wooden steps in those days—and the nurses were
against it. He even tried to hit, a little lamely, with the walking stick against
the small of their legs. But because his thoughts or impulses were never of
long consequence he was not difficult to keep under control, and the nurses
had plenty of time to exchange conversation about the little intermezzo while
they were still walking. The older and more experienced nurse was of the
opinion that previously, that is to say, "in life," he was accustomed to turning
off just there, to walk that way, and that it was "still there." This, that in his
presence they undisturbedly discussed what habits he might have had "in
life," made a deep impression on me.

During this time he stirred and dredged in a low voice, but in a discontented
and disputatious fashion. There were no words, for it was rather unarticulated,
but what one could clearly hear was the "intonation" of the sentences. The
words had disappeared but the intonation had remained, and it could be mod-

ulated and modified in several ways. What I best recall is that brooding tone. The other room from the salon I just described was my room and it too looked out on the street. It had an inner door to the toilet and the bathroom that was a throughway with the main door to the bedroom corridor. On the toilet he would often sit for hours and mumble in the endless, longbrooding rigamarole, sometimes in a rising tone like a self defense, sometimes in a sinking tone as if he tried to understand the intrigue behind the whole thing, or perhaps as if he went through items in a ledger, or discussed business. Since the toilet was placed right in front of my door, I could hear all this very well, but what I myself did I have forgotten. Perhaps I looked at picture books or played; perhaps I faltered and spelled already in the ABC book, for I had begun to read with a governess. Of that ABC book I remember clearly and precisely the reference "NOSE," where the word nose stood in capital and small printed letters and in script, illustrated with a clumsy picture of a dognose (without eyes, ears or the rest that properly belonged.) What a dognose was I knew very well for I had had a beloved collie named Guerre, but I could never get any connection between these letters and that fragmentary picture; and that incomprehensibility has in some way coupled together in my memory with that muttering from the other side of the door.

Other, more naïve souls had, however, in their way a different attitude about his condition. The cook and the housemaid, who were both "saved," alleged, when much later they talked about it, that while cleaning in the little salon they spoke with him about his faith and that he confessed his and "was so happy" and "felt so good." This must naturally be understood as one of the manic outbreaks of happiness which normally follow the breakdown.

From the library, between my own room and the salon, I remember too how he used me as an oracle. He let me open up a bible or opened it up himself and let me point. That he opened it himself seems most probable, because I still have that bible and it is only in Psalms that he made marginal markings and underlinings according to this oracle method. "Take sword and shield and stand up for me; draw forth the spear and stop my persecutors. Say to my soul: 'I am your salvation.'" What sort of information he could get from that I do not know, but it probably verifies that all oracles are obscure. In the margin in pencil there is written: "11/9 1913 4-6 (7 is crossed out) acc. to G.E."

But that is a memory from a markedly healthier period, relatively speaking, before he sank further down into night. Of such more or less healthy memories I have only a few: a couple of scenes from the office at Peace Street: one time I had run into one of the monstrous, at that time, forward rattling cars and went in my pants from outright terror; the other time I sat and played with several one and two penny coins and got to know, after asking, that it was so large a coin (a two penny piece) that he earned per day, which worried me and made me feel sorry for him. Why? Because I probably knew that it was very little money. What futile memories often fasten first and last the longest.

A third memory from Lönas estate comes from a wild appearance on the bottom floor which could be heard all the way up and in which he guaranteed "that he could piss in the pot" that such and such a fact was true. It concerned a sore on his elbow (hard underneath) which he claimed to have gotten when he banged it on the bathtub and no other way. But that can be something which I snapped up later and coupled together with the memory of the bottom floor scene. I remember, however, that one of his more solid acquaintances, a Lieutenant W., was along, and that a carriage from Stockholm, a high box-looking black thing waited in the distance where the road hooked into the forest. I could see it from the front gable window and it seemed to me a portent of bad luck. That probably was one of the last and definitive breakdowns.

But even afterward, on the basis of a peculiar piety, when he was calm sometimes, he got "to sit at the table," an expression which was otherwise used for children. He got a big napkin tied around his neck and I remember that he ate eggs in a very unpleasant way so that the yolk ran down over his chin. Once he went in his pants and there must have been something extremely powerful in the urine for the expensive light red Milanese brocade on one of the chairs still bears a light blue, litmus colored spot. That is why in my photograph he sits in his rococo armchair on a layer of folded in quadruple blankets.

Often he was sent away to one or another sanitorium or hospital, but just as often he came home again, for the same piety which decided that he should eat with us at the breakfast table decided also that he was better off at home. I myself was often sent in turn to children's homes, where for that matter I was never materially uncomfortable. And besides childhood is such that even the most rejected and pathetic one always has some light memories to offer, for it needs so little: a glade with sun, unknown flowers and animals, the country, fun on a beach can quickly cover over the stranger and the strangeness. But loneliness at night with all kinds of terrifying images and among strangers, yes, even in a children's home the longing for letters or a sign of life can give aches as fully developed in the child's soul as in adults, perhaps more, for the child has his own powerlessness drawn into it.

Ester was the name of my Glumdalclitch in the giant's world, the only soft motherly being I knew during those years, a pilot's daughter who sometimes worked at our house and at whose house I sometimes stayed. She married later a poor archipelago priest and both were killed one stormy night when she went with him to visit a dying man. Even Guerre was sold and he mourned so deeply that he ran away from the new owner and was never found.

Later I got to see my father as a corpse. Gangrene set in, or at least so I was instructed to say to eventual questions, that it was gangrene. He did not resemble himself in the coffin. He seemed completely strange. When one sees a man long since undone become truly definitively undone, the contrast seems even greater, perhaps because the border has long been so wavering. He did not haunt long. But he still haunts.

The Sunset

From a Romantic's Notes

I stand on a height and look in to the land. Beneath me trees dream with heavy crowns of dusk. The glades lie empty. Nothing living is seen: there are no roads here. But whenever they wish flying forest-beings flicker past in the shadows below, disappear again . . . A dog's echoing bark reaches me from the distance, a remote trumpet call . . . It is the sun that sinks.

The evening around me is full of mirages. The sky burns. Long do I want to stand here, to look out at the bluing forests where I have wandered in darkness, without finding the road, without knowing myself.

I turn around toward the sea, see how the sun gives it over to the twilight. Like a single golden grain hidden in purple smoke, nearly unnoticeable, the Star continues to shine between the small golden clouds. I thought I heard music that slowly died. As always my goal is distant.

I climb slowly down the mountain, without moving. Dew falls in the glades, glimmers in spiders' webs. When I walk in under the trees I get spider webs on my forehead, mouth, and eyes. It is like sleeping. The trees too are enchanted. Rare fruits hang hidden among the leaves, eyes that secretly see me, ears that hear me come . . .

There, beyond the forest's edge moving darkly in its dream, the sea, restless as a sleeping man with a light upon his face . . . It is the stars that light one by one.

The night and the moon have come when I leave the forest. A stray flake of wind searches among the last trees, perhaps after someone who hid or someone who disappeared. As I walk along the beach I find cold kindling, ashes spread out. The breakers surge indistinctly; the stones glisten damp and cold in the wave-swell after a long defeated storm. The horizon still looms weakly.

I walk further around the cape. Deep in the inlet a firelight meets me. It comes closer and closer. Now I see that the fire burns in a cave. Dark figures flicker around it. Are they shepherds or wanderers?

I walk slowly forward. One of them works with something, moves slowly back and forth over the stone walls. The others sit silent and still with their lips tightly closed on something, as if they carried a secret on their tongues.

It is like sorcery. What is it they hide in their mouths? I know that it is the last pebble; I see the staffs leaning against the cliff; I knew that I should find them here. This is another beach: I could not have gone in a circle. It is here that one embarks.

2

Someone speaks:

I remember, I came from the distant land, but that is a long time now: I did not even know myself. I must have been someone else. Have I crossed over so many borders and through so many shadows that I gradually became someone else? Or have I dreamed the whole thing? But that would be neither a solace nor a riddle's answer: dreams are also life's destiny.

I must have been someone else and yet I am not conscious of any change. The essential is left: the goal, my movement's direction. It is like life! When did I notice that I had changed? Would I have recognized myself fifteen years ago?

No, I am no longer afraid of changes. Changes are simplifications. I would have recognized myself and I would not have recognized myself.

It is the irrevocable to which one day we must succeed in giving expression. The storms help us forward in the direction toward it, but calms bury and delay us. The calm, that is death, the ink on man's foot; the tar he sticks in. Either death does not exist or it is nothing other than the great delay, the hell that stones live in—for everything lives.

I am afraid of stupidity and inertia. I do not want to be left behind. If we could escape these meaningless back lessons, if we could escape these endless catechisms and learn only one hundred words of the supraearthly language, then everything we had to say would soon be said. Then we would cease having to fight for every word.

In one way or another I have since come to know that this was the first time I came to earth. It is possible, otherwise why should I feel so alien here? There are men who immediately and without thinking find their place in life. They say, "My life is real; your life is unreal—I walk here; why do you walk there?" It is such men who have been here a long time without getting anywhere, such men who stick in the tar and make their beds in the slough and make themselves comfortably at home. Reality, thus, should be to argue about taste: my reality is more real than yours and vice versa. No matter how much I have let books and men cheat me—none has yet succeeded in getting me to believe in reality. There is no reality. At best there is a will to reality, and that is evil until man has learned to count on the brain's and the heart's misguiding.

No, I hated their indifference, their annoying way of making etiquette of everything and believing themselves ready with the world and with themselves. I remember with what pleasure they used to point to Greek moderation—mediocrity it became in their mouths. But which of them has understood the divine dream that lay concealed in the words, "but not too much?" One must have long been immoderate in order to reach that point.

We must not relax. Have we learned to experience the kingdom of death deeply enough; have we seen so many glimpses of heaven that we can make even the palest representation of it? Have we longed and strained enough in moderation? No, not us and even less the others. Not until then shall we be worthy; not until then shall we be noble enough. Not until the last beach shall we be able to look into the sunset with something of equality's melancholy. Not until tranquil, free from exaggeration and sickness shall we take our places in the new kingdom.

But first through the fire! The devil must be driven out through hell, the measureless thirst for beauty must be quenched and the drunkenness in our veins transformed to sobriety clear into the heart. Let us burn, let the frenzy cool, let the ashes fly with the wind. Perhaps a bird shall be born from the fire and lift itself toward the other land where the sunset is the sunrise.

I took life seriously and distrusted the I, the little daily will and life of the moment. I did not lose the feeling for the meaningful which otherwise occurs: I thought I knew that "I" was another, that life's deepest streams always evaded the conscious-now-I, the near-sighted near. Our now is seldom more than a certain selfish absent-mindedness: it is only love sometimes and art sometimes that give us the possibility to gather life's, the past and the coming, weight into a moment.

But that is the exception. We are dead in ourselves and unborn in ourselves. It is in the past and the future that we live, in wish and in memory . . .

3

I remember I came from the distant land, but that is a long time now: I did not even know myself. I remember . . . It is like looking down into a pool with brown water, filled with tadpoles, red ringed worms, curious small protozoa, mosquito larvae, dragonfly larvae, and other larvae, but mostly tadpoles.

Much later, in one of the big cities, I was awakened one night by invisible voices. I tried to defend myself against them, tried vainly to convince them to leave me to my fate. Finally I found myself in a state of peculiar excitement.

It was as if I had heard a once well-known language to which I had lost the key. They were friendly, helpful voices which at any price seemed to want to warn me, to teach me something that could not be delayed. But it was so difficult for them to make themselves understood in their language. I had to strain my entire concentration in order to grasp specific words and sentences: "Upward to the west," where I came from. And then I seemed to see a desert of human-looking stones. It was "hell which neared the earth from the southeast where the plane curves." This plane would be transparent so that one could look down: I had been there and seen . . . Or something in that style.

For several hours they talked around me: in other words, my memory was profoundly revitalized.

What an odd mood in the room! The high window crossings white against the darkness; the light which shone reticently in the night, and there, in the shimmering brass bed, she who always used to sleep while I watched . . . It swayed around me. I thought I could see over the endless water surface. Sleep lay far off like a fogbank over a sea. The stars were eyes which looked at me—there were no real stars. And I myself sat as awake as the radioman on some disabled steamer: as if everything depended on me. The whole time a swarm of voices and furthest away one lone voice that sought to reach me, that fought to make itself heard. The words reached me distorted, nearly incomprehensible. It was as if against my will I was forced to hear incorrectly—as if another I of myself had forbidden me to hear.

The foggy winter dawn's angels sat on my window frame and looked for a long time out into the empty air with their rainclear eyes before I knew in myself: the earth is the worms' kingdom, a blind and crawling throng of larvae which give birth to larvae but rarely a butterfly. And soon the world's winter is here. Fly into the sunset you autumn's last butterflies with burning wings. Believe in your longing that the fire is good. Soon it will be dangerous not to dare!

I remember, I came from the distant land. I had travelled long in the night; it began to dawn.

Then I noticed that I walked arm in arm with someone but it was as if we had not really been wakened, neither she nor I, as if we still dreamed.

We went arm in arm in a gigantic room. It was a museum, but the walls rose completely empty. There was nothing other than a shadowlike, immense stranger, continually the same. The room was filled with a gray green twilight, curiously translucent. One could see how he streamed around like the circulation of blood, inescapable and always counter-clockwise. And we two who walked clockwise met him continuously anew. Then he stretched his terrible, expressionless, threatening face toward us, always the same, quite near . . .

I pressed closer to her side in fear. I did not want to lose her—and anyway I lost her. At the exit I was alone, I do not know how . . . I was alone in the purple desert where there was no human besides myself. The purple desert was blood-red as the sunset. It sloped slowly upward. One trudged heavily in the deep sand—and there, on the other side of the summit the end of the world happened!

Then it came about that I was alone in the world, just as alone as a child in a crowd of people in the park and whom no policeman can soothe. It was the first time I came to the earth. We were separated from each other already at the entrance to the world. I have looked for her everywhere.

4

I remember a long and rumbling darkness, perhaps a tunnel—and suddenly one came out of it and saw through the window stony inclines, dwarfed pines, sharp cliffs, an ice sea, floating, snowwhite mountain tops, all equally distant and all equally near. Also a birth. All around me black-clad people arose, pointed with gloved hands and called: "Die Jungfrau . . ." I imagined since then that it was a girl in a checkered, armless dress, walking a forest path with a basket in her hand. But I could not see her and could not understand why they called so loudly.

I remember the surface of a sagalike lake glittering blue white through a cast iron gate. On both sides the balcony was divided by screens with voices coming from each side . . . Someone liked me, I do not know any longer who. I turned my back and looked out over the lake. But one could not lean over the gate: then came the dizziness. Only look there occasionally and cautiously.

I remember a snake that lifted its head over the heather and looked at me, curious, not evilly. Then it lay down again and wriggled away.

I remember a darkness which fell over the earth. It was mid-day when the birds stopped singing and sat amazed and suddenly heavy with sleep on their branches. It became murky under the trees, it smelled of dusk in the thicket of ferns. And the darkness sank slowly over the earth like flocks of twilight-colored snow. Something happened in the sky, magic powers played games, it was like walking in a dream. One could not look up, then one was blinded.

I remember a birdling that lay in the road. It slept with the fine white membrane of dream over its eye and leaned its head softly toward the ground like a pillow. I thought it a pity that the bird slept in the middle of the road and could be run over, not because it was dead. I wanted to lift it up, but something held me back, turned it with a stick. Then I saw it was filled with white living maggots.

I remember one time when I was near the earth that I did not hurt myself when I fell. The stones were friendly to me. The trees protected me. But I was afraid of the ants. "Go to the anthill and learn . . ." Gradually I learned to hurt myself and be afraid.

I also remember one evening in a coast town with salty twilight winds. We ran after a windwheel on dusky streets, far out in the country. From the meadow that sloped up toward the new moon could be heard children's songs. A little fisherman's girl was mine in the game. I felt her warm breath near my ear when she whispered . . . the word.

I remember a lake where we bathed. The water was brown and stinging in the eyes. If one swam out a way he hit a big rock under the water. It was as much fun and as terrifying as a sea serpent. Beyond the inlet was the girl's cove. I looked over there. There she stood in the water's edge, hesitating, waiting for the others. Her nakedness overpowered me: the hips already wide, the beautiful even brown skin, the childishly pale lips within her pelvis, the very young breasts. She stood completely still, hesitating, waiting for the courage to go in. I never knew her but I know her.

I remember a little park at the corner of an immense rushing street. A Punch and Judy show shrilled near by. Punch hit the Kaiser on the head with his cudgel—whack—whack—whack! And everyone laughed. Little girls with skirts that barely hid their panties came riding by, on gray clumping donkeys, spraddling and kicking with naked bony legs. One wanted to pull their legs.

Small red cars buzzed past in endless rows with corks in the radiators. Red and yellow drinks shone mistily in glasses, on the table under spring's tree. And the world's biggest postage stamp was mine.

But around the corner slyly smiling sneaked the old woman who stole children.

Why should the stranger always pursue me, why did I never get home? The well-known door—I knew where it was, but someone or something hindered me and held me back . . .

And why did all the roads lead me so far from myself?

The realm of wishes . . . I saw it before me and ran there but it was never the same.

The girl on the beach . . . Why could not we have been together as we were, in simplicity?

The whole longed for land of childhood . . . Sunrise over the troll lake, the hot fragrant hill of wild strawberries in the midday sun, the bells in the forest and the clear, echoing voices around the lake in the evening . . . And the simplicity and happiness of being—here and nowhere else.

Why cannot I go back there? Why could not I stay there?

Now all that is remote as if I had never lived. I live poisoned in an anthill and all that remains for me is to follow the line, to drive out the devil with hell. When that is gone, some time, and far from here, perhaps I shall walk into a land similar to the old one.

5

The years went by. One time I went home. The well-known door opened and I went into the little room with my eyes looking down to the floor. There he sat, the stranger, the sick man. His face shone joyfully when he saw me. Rays of sun played in the room.

Hello little grandpa, he said. Grandpa is here, hello little grandpa, come here little grandpa . . .

He moved a little in his chair, smiled a light and bewildered smile. The nurse smiled too but coldly and habitually. Both their smiles were equally strange. Her stepmotherly guarding motions when she straightened the blanket embarrassed me and made me sad. One could not show that one was sad in front of the stranger.

Outside the bells boomed. The sunset glowed in the window. A last ray fell in the room, played on the wall. What should I say and do? "He called me 'grandpa.'" I thumbed my cap.

The clear moments were so rare. Otherwise he was usually far away. His face had an absent and decayed expression and his lips mumbled continually incomprehensible words which he got from far away.

—He hears voices, they said to me, and I understood. I did not know that it was only a manner of speaking.

For years he was as someone whom one has already said goodby to, someone one recently has been separated from and who goes his way and whose face becomes more and more indistinct, soon a disappearing memory.

And the years went by. I lived as before under the peal of the heavy bells. They woke me often in the mornings. It was like waking out of a deep and funereal dream. They pursued me long into the mournful winter twilight. It was always someone who died so that they could ring.

Sometimes doubt came and grabbed me by the hair. I knotted my hands but did not stamp on the floor, only became more alone. No one understood me—it was a common complaint but I had an honest reason: I did not understand myself.

I remember how I used to open the window secretly and climb up the chimney steps to the ridge of the roof. The city lay beneath me and the sunset bled over the furthest roofs. All the city's bells tolled funerals across the world and I myself was filled with that most sorrowful music.

To fly in the sunset. Melancholy blood-red was my color since childhood and I wallowed in the thought that everyone was going to die and I would be left alone in the world. What an opportunity to be finally completely drowned in sweet self-pity. Or too I imagined that, lamented, I died and returned to a distant land. The roof lifted and swayed. I fluttered my wings. But I did not want to fall down. I wanted to fly into the sunset and burn there. For a long time it was like flying into the past, to bury myself in sorrow's beautiful blood-red earth.

One day I shall free myself of excess, one day time shall adjust me to myself. Success is a lesson, no fairy gift. Are moderation and humility the right means to go forward? No, they are goals, not means. We cannot go unto death with preserved energies. Perhaps fatigue's poison may kill most people, but a few it will heal, and I want to know if I am among them. Gladly I will gamble my self if I know that perhaps I can win my self. That kind of life strikes me as more worthy than the half-way and the indolent.

The years went and the bells silenced one by one. I stared into the sunset with my entire soul. My attention became soundless. The Star was lit in silence, shining nearly unnoticeably over the desert. And like an echo nearly inaudible an endless music reached me.

Had I matured? Had I memorized the first chapter already? And was it no longer the past that I saw, but the future? What reward, to feel oneself on a good and right way.

Since then I have listened to the music from many heights and beaches. I have gone through darknesses. Half-blind and nearly unconscious I have beaten my way forward, to the west. And every time I reached a clear perspective it seemed in any case as if the goal was nearer. Blood-red is no longer my color. I have found gold. Real gold is worthless. I stand once again on a beach where I can breathe out and think about what memories I shall take with me across the sea.*

* In the 1963 Delfin edition of *Promenades and Excursions*, the text of which is somewhat revised, Ekelöf added:

6

The shadows flutter over the stone walls. The staffs lean against the rock. The fire is mirrored in their still eyes. None of the others have moved.

Open it, Write

I

Of life, of the living,
Of death, of the dead.
Of love and hate.
Of east and west,
the two that never shall meet
and never separate
but be aware of the other's nearness,
know and follow the other's movements,
as man must do
in hate and in love.

I sing of the only thing that can redeem,
the only practical, the same for all:
How seldom man holds the power
to renounce power!
To renounce the I and its voice, renounce—
this alone gives power.

II

I rise up out of my ashes
—thought and emotional life
on the way to being swallowed by the formless wave

again I float over.
Only as witnesses do men exist:
Make it your own, and write!
There is no strength other than inner strength
that from the outer comes
from that mysterious thing that moves up there
shines through those vaguely self-lit clouds
streams over you in its galvanic force
so that you feel yourself wrestling!
Then it is the power wrestling, not you!
How does the power wrestle?
There is no weakness other than inner weakness
that from the outer comes
from that mysterious thing that moves down there
shape-shifting, dark-bulging,

threatening, magnetic.
You feel the strong arms wrestle!
Then it is the power wrestling, not you!
How does the power wrestle?
Truly, you are no more than an arena!
A wanderer the sun and storm strip bare
at once! Not turn and turn about.
Icecold in shade, redhot in the sun.
The soul's April.

III

You say "I" and "it is about me"
but it is about a bet:
In reality you are no one.
So I-less, naked and formless is the real!
It was in fear of it that you began to wear clothes,
began to behave yourself and call yourself "I,"
hold fast to a straw.
In reality you are no one.
Judicial system, human dignity, free will,
all are pictures painted out of fear in reality's empty halls,
fear of confessing something beyond right and wrong, beyond thesis and
antithesis!

In reality you are no one.
Yourself beyond good and evil an arena of good and evil,
The beast above fighting the beast below—
You may be aware of truth, an abyss at the roadside,
not daring to know, unwilling to know,
you who go dizzy at the smallest pit!
In reality you are no one.
Your suit; a place, a name—
all else is merely your wish,
your "I" a wish, your lostness one, your savedness another:
you have taken it all out in advance!

Saved, there is no saved! You dream up "saved"
and stammer Arisen! and Holy!—for this is your wish.
And man's condition stands unchangeably firm
but you have reached the next stage in your edifice of wish
Yet a wish of all the conceivable thousands and thousands
has become possible, necessary to you, certain and finally fact,
like yourself, also a wish from the beginning,
like the magical name your parents gave you

to shield you from darkness and egolessness,
to distinguish you from thousands alike and almost alike.
And yet you are at the root nameless as night and the dark:
In reality you are no one.

IV

The beauty I sought till now was the springboard's vibration.
The wisdom I knew till now was the cowardice of the diver.
But he who expects redemption, he is the unredeemed,
He who wants salvation, he is already damned.
Denial? No, the profoundest faith,
the one that can be owned when you believe in nothing
the one that can be owned only when you know:
I do lie not, there is no lie in me
and truth is far from me (I am far from me).
I abandon me
as the last rat abandons the sinking ship,
the burning wreck, and the deep gets its share, when the heights have theirs,
(you are weighed and found to weigh part light, part heavy),
a shipwrecked man who drifts in the shape-shifting dark,
attracted and lit by the star of mysterious war,
she who unseen is stronger than sun and moon,
she who at once is single and double, dark and light,
at once! Not by turn and turn about.
Life is where opposites meet,
Life is neither side.
Life is neither day nor night
but daybreak and twilight.
Life is neither evil nor good,
it is the meal between millstones.
Life is not the battle of the dragon and the knight,
it is the virgin.
And let no one tell me of the dragon's hunger and rage
and let no one tell me of the knight's magnanimity,
although the tales lie beautifully!

And let no one tell me of the virgin's trust and hope,
for the battle lasts forever
and the one who will surrender life
is not the dragon
and not the knight
but always the virgin.

V

The virgin's anguish and flight are the sword and the claws.
Of her flight and anguish is the sword hammered and the sharp claws grown.
She dies every moment, therefore she lives.
She flees every moment, therefore she endures.
She stores up power and counter-power, therefore she sways.
She sways, therefore she is in balance.
The crown, the mantle, and the clasped hands belong to the battle, not to her,
but the battle belongs to her.
Through her the battle exists:
She is its decoy.

O deep calm, wrapped in storm!
You are a doll, left behind by children,
will-less, you yield to empty action!
You emerge for the one who penetrates the battle.
You vanish before the one who discovers you
for he disappears in you:
A door that opens, a road that wanders away.
On the way, a single shape diminishing.
The same shape that wanders off and disappears,
again and again the same
who again and again disappears:
Illusion and virgin birth.

> translated by
> Muriel Rukeyser and Leif Sjöberg

The Gymnosophist

What I mean
what I want
is something else
always something else—

Man's external conditions
Now, here, only this, the fact
Man's internal conditions:
Whenever, only not now
wherever, only not here
whatever, only not this—

What is it then that I want? What is it I mean?
I know what it is—and I do not know!
It has no name, no place, no kind
I cannot call for it, not explain it
It is that which gets its name when I call
It is that which gets meaning when I explain
That is it—but before I have yet called
That is it—but before I have yet explained
It is that which still has no name
That which has a name is not something else—

It is a step forward before I take it
It is a step backward when I take it
It is a step to the side before I take it
It is a step to the other side when I take it
It is immediately above my head before I lift it
and when I lift it it is immediately beneath my foot
It is like the insect the swallow hunts in the air
It is like the swallow the insect is hunted by
It is where I was, it was where I am
Who knows? Who knows? Who knows?
That is what I know
standing here on one leg in the swamp:
Holy is God Life, holy is God Death
in the power of God Something Else
the four headed divinity's both profiles
in the power of his halfness, in the power of his half invisibility
in the power of his turned-away face
in the power of God Something Else

[144]

unseen, invisible, untaught in writing
anyway everywhere named although unnamed
everywhere known although unknown!

Unholy alone is God Fact
he who turns his face to us
in the power of the other two's half-invisibility in visibility worshipped
like God Life, like God Death
but holy, holy, alone holy in the power of himself is God
God Something Else!

And still there is the greatest secrecy
elsewhere preserved
always elsewhere—

Oh heron, oh stork, oh flamingo
you would-be-wise birds
standing here around me in the dawn's hour
among waking flowers
standing here on one leg in the swamp.

Absentia Animi

In Autumn
In autumn of your leave-taking
In autumn when all gates stand open to meaningless pastures
where unreal mushrooms go rotten
and water filled wheel-tracks are heading
to nothing, and a snail is heading to
a frayed butterfly is heading
to nothing, which is a faded rose
the smallest and ugliest. And the insects, stupid devils
brittle-legged, drunk in lamplight in the evening
and the lamp itself sighing sinking
about the zero of the sea of light, thought's polar ocean
with its long waves
quietly seething foam
of series divided by series
of nothing through nothing to nothing
thesis antithesis synthesis abrasax abraxas Thesis
(like the sound of a sewing-machine)
And spiders spin their webs across the silent night
and cicadas scrape
Meaningless.

Unreal. Meaningless

    In autumn

My poem rustles
Words do their work and lie there
Dust rains over them, dust or dew
till the wind whirls up and lays (them) there (and) elsewhere
he who partout seeks the meaning of all things has long since realized
that the meaning with the rustling is the rustling
which in itself is something other than
wet rubbers through leaves
absent-minded footsteps on the park's carpet
of leaves, affectionately adhering
to wet rubbers, absent-minded steps
You are lost, most lost
Don't be in such a hurry
Wait a while
Wait
In autumn when
In autumn when all gates

it so happens that in the last slanting ray
> after a day of rain
> with long pauses hesitating
> > as if caught in the act

an overlooked blackbird sings in a treetop
for nothing, for the throat's sake. And you see
his treetop standing against the sky's pale background
close to a single cloud. And the cloud swims
like other clouds, but also overlooked, hors saison
essentially long ago and somewhere else
and in itself (like the song) already other than

Eternal rest
Meaningless. Unreal.
> Meaningless. I
sing sit here
of the sky of a cloud
I wish nothing more
I wish myself far far away
I am far away (among evening echoes)
I am here
Thesis antithesis abrasax
You also I
O far far away
swims in the bright sky
over a treetop a cloud
in happy unconsciousness!
O deep down in me
the eye of black pearl reflects from its surface
in happy half-consciousness
the image of a cloud!
Not a thing that exists
It is something else
It is in something existent
but it does not exist
It is something else
O far far away
in what is beyond is found
something very near!
O deep down in me
in that which is near
is something beyond
something beyond-near

in what is near and far
something neither-nor
in what is either-or:
neither cloud nor image
neither image nor image
neither cloud nor cloud
neither neither nor nor
but something else !
The only thing that is
is something else !
The only thing that is
in that which is
is something else !
The only thing that is
in this which is
is that which in this
is something else !
(O the soul's cradle-song
the song of something else !)

O

non sens
non sentiens non
dissentiens
indesinenter
terque quaterque
pluries
vox
vel abracadabra

Abraxas abrasax
Thesis antithesis synthesis which again becomes thesis
      Meaningless.
Unreal. Meaningless.

And spiders spin their webs across the silent night
cicadas scrape
                    In Autumn

                              translated by
                              Muriel Rukeyser and Leif Sjöberg

BIBLIOGRAPHY

BOOKS BY GUNNAR EKELÖF

(All the books listed below were published by Bonniers, Stockholm, Sweden, with the exception of the first two listed, which were published by Spekstrum, Stockholm.)

Sent på jorden, 1932
Fransk surrealism, 1933
Dedikation, 1934
Hundra år modern fransk dikt, 1934
Sorgen och stjärnan, 1936
Köp den blindes sång, 1938
Färjesång, 1941
Promenader, 1941
Non serviam, 1945
Utflykter, 1947
Dikter, 1949
Om hösten, 1951
Strountes, 1955
Dikter 1932-51, 1956
Blandade kort, 1957
Verklighetsflykt. Valda promenader och utflykter, 1958
Opus incertum, 1959
Valfrändskaper, 1960
En Mölna-Elegi, 1960
En natt i Otocac, 1961
Sent på jorden med Appendix 1962 och En Natt Vid Horisonten, 1962
Diwan över Fursten av Emgión, 1965
Dikter, 1965
Sagan om Fatumeh, 1966
Vägvisare till underjorden, 1967

POSTHUMOUSLY PUBLISHED

Lägga patience, 1969
Partitur, 1969

WORKS SPECIFICALLY PERTAINING TO GUNNAR EKELÖF

(In general this bibliography identifies only material referred to in this study. A definitive bibliography has been published by Reidar Ekner, and I strongly recommend it to anyone concerned with literature by or about Gunnar Ekelöf.)

[149]

Bergsten, Gunilla. "Abraxas: Ett motiv hos Herman Hesse och Gunnar Ekelöf." *Samlaren*, årg. 85, 1964.

———. "Abraxas. Gunnar Ekelöf: Absentia Animi." *Svenska Diktanalyser*. Ed. M. von Platen. Stockholm: Prisma/FIBs lyrikklub, 1965.

Ekner, Reidar. "Gunnar Ekelöf: Panthoidens sång." *Att läsa poesi*. Ö. Lindberger and R. Ekner. Stockholm: Verdandis skriftserie, 1955.

———. "Tradition och egenart hos Gunnar Ekelöf." *En bok om Gunnar Ekelöf*. Stockholm, 1956.

———. "Vårt hjärtas klubbslag vid Jarama." *Ord och Bild*, årg. 74, 1965.

———. "Ekelöfs akritcykel." *BLM*, årg. 34, 1965.

———. *I den havandes liv. Åtta kapitel om Gunnar Ekelofs lyrik*. Stockholm: Bonniers, 1967.

———. "Herren Någonting Annat. Drömmen om Indien hos Gunnar Ekelöf." *Ord och Bild*, årg. 76, 1967.

———. "Det mörknar över vägen." *Svensk Litteraturtidskrift*. Vol. 31. 1968.

———. *Gunnar Ekelöf—En bibliografi*. Stockholm: Bonniers, 1970.

Enckell, Rabbe. "Det omvända perspektivet." *Prisma*, årg. 3, 1950.

Espmark, Kjell. "Den brokiga muren." *BLM*, 1959.

———. "Ekelöf och Eliot. En studie kring Färjesång." *BLM*, årg. 28, 1959.

Lindegren, Erik. "Gunnar Ekelöf: en modern mystiker." *Kritiskt 40-tal*. Ed. K. Vennberg and W. Aspenström. Stockholm, 1948.

———. "På väg mot instrumentallyriken." *Kritiskt 40-tal*. Ed. K. Vennberg and W. Aspenström. Stockholm, 1948.

Printz-Påhlson, Göran. "Diktarens kringkastade lemmar." *Solen i spegeln*. Stockholm, 1958.

Sjöberg, Leif. "Gunnar Ekelöf's 'Tag och skriv,' a reader's commentary." *Scandinavian Studies*, vol. 25, no. 4, 1963.

Tigerschiöld, Brita. "Samothrakes tema." *BLM*, årg, 28 1959.

Wigforss, Brita (Tigerschiöld). "Ekelöf vid horisonten." *BLM*, årg. 32, March, 1963.

General Reference Material

Bachelard, Gaston. *La Terre et les rêveries du repos*. Paris: J. Corti, 1948.

———. *L'Eau et les rêves: Essai sur l'imagination de la matière*. Paris: Corti, 1942.

———. *La Terre et les rêveries de la volonté*. Paris: Corti, 1948.

———. *The Poetics of Space*. Trans. M. Jolas. New York: Orion Press, 1964.

Baudouin, Charles. *Psychoanalysis and Aesthetics*. Trans. E. C. Paul. New York: Dodd, Mead, 1924.

Bodkin, Maud. *Archetypal Patterns in Poetry: Psychological Studies of Imagination*. London: Oxford University Press, 1951.

Breton, André. *Manifestes du surréalisme*. Paris: nrf, Gallimard, 1966.

Brown, Norman O. *Love's Body*. New York: Random House, 1966.

Geijerstam, Carl-Erik. *Det Personliga Experimentet.* Stockholm: Bonniers, 1963.

Jacobi, Jolande. *The Way of Individuation.* Trans. R. F. C. Hull. New York: Harcourt, Brace and World, 1967.

Jung, Carl Gustaf. *The Structure and Dynamics of the Psyche.* Trans. R. F. C. Hull. New York: Bollingen, 1960.

———. *Psychology and Alchemy.* New York: Bollingen Series 20, 1953.

Jung, Carl Gustaf, and C. Kerenyi. *Essays on a Science of Mythology.* Trans. R. F. C. Hull. New York: Bollingen Series 22, 1949.

Linder, Erik Hjalmar. *Ny Illustrerad Svensk Litteraturhistoria.* Vol. 5. Stockholm: Natur och Kultur, 1958.

Serrano, Miguel. *C. G. Jung and Hermann Hesse.* Trans. Frank MacShane. London: Routledge and K. Paul, 1966.

Sewell, Elizabeth. *The Orphic Voice.* New Haven: Yale University Press, 1960.

Ziolkowski, Theodore. *The Novels of Hermann Hesse.* Princeton: Princeton University Press, 1965.